MW01142026

THE JESUS ENCOUNTER

THE JESUS ENCOUNTER

STORIES *of* PEOPLE *in* *the* BIBLE WHO MET JESUS

WILLIAM TINSLEY

GRAND RAPIDS, MICHIGAN 49530

We want to hear from you. Please send your comments about this book to us in care of the address below. Thank you.

GRAND RAPIDS, MICHIGAN 49530

www.zondervan.com

ZONDERVAN™

The Jesus Encounter

First Zondervan Edition 2002

Requests for information should be addressed to:

Zondervan, *Grand Rapids, Michigan 49530*

Library of Congress Cataloging-in-Publication Data

Tinsley, William C.
The Jesus encounter : stories of people in the Bible who met Jesus / William Tinsley.
p. cm.
Includes bibliographical references and index.
ISBN 0-310-24330-0
1. Bible. N.T.—Biography. 2. Jesus Christ—Friends and associates.
I. Title.
BS2430 .T56 2001
232.9—dc21 2001045577

This edition printed on acid-free paper.

Interior design by Nancy Wilson

Printed in the United States of America

02 03 04 05 06 07 08 09 /❖ DC/ 10 9 8 7 6 5 4 3 2 1

To

Jonathan

Collin

Allison

CONTENTS

THIS BOOK IS DEDICATED TO MY CHILDREN, JONATHAN, COLLIN, and Allison, members of the next generation who inherit the age-old story, which must be passed on. They have gratified my heart and filled me with pleasure as I observe their faith in Jesus Christ during their youth and young adulthood. I am confident the story is secure in their hands.

I wish to express special thanks to Gomer Lesch for voluntarily serving as my teacher and mentor in writing. He has tirelessly edited volumes of my writing, which poured into his email, patiently pointing out corrections while always encouraging me to continue.

I must also thank Charles Lee Williamson, who not only serves as a counselor and friend, but exemplifies indefatigable entrepreneurship that refuses to consider defeat in any goal. His example inspired the steps to see this volume in print.

And, as always, I am grateful to my wife, Jackie, with whom I have shared a lifelong encounter with Jesus. Our wedding song has been our lifelong prayer, "Saviour, Like a Shepherd Lead Us."

WILLIAM TINSLEY KNOWS JESUS; HE DOES NOT JUST KNOW ABOUT him. And he knows about those persons who were close to Jesus during his ministry on earth because he is a devout student of the Bible. Those two factors combined with Tinsley's gift of communication and insight into human nature have produced one of the most moving, inspiring books of our day.

The personalities of the New Testament who encountered Jesus come alive on these pages. Nothing else available really accomplishes this. Movies have been made about these persons but often they are not true to the biblical record. Church dramas and pageants portray these persons but such efforts, sincere as they may be, often fall short of reality.

The persons chronicled in these pages come alive because Tinsley does not describe them so much as he provides a means for each to tell his or her story in the first person. Thus he allows us to see Jesus as they saw him, to experience Jesus as they experienced him. Jesus becomes more real to us as do those who tell the story of their encounter with him.

Each account is based on the Bible's record. Where the author ventures beyond the account in the Bible, he says so. The monologues also reflect careful research into the various facets of life during New Testament times. The reader will discover new insight into familiar stories as they are based on factual material. The customs of the day, the horror of crucifixion, the manner of burial—all these and more fill these pages, carefully woven into the monologues so as not to distract but to illustrate.

The writing is clear, simple, and yet profound. The descriptions of persons and events are so vividly written that one feels as if he or she were an eyewitness. Beautiful phrases make this work of prose almost seem like poetry.

The monologues are not limited to utilizing the words of these personalities recorded in Scripture. The author utilizes dedicated imagination in putting words in the mouths and minds of each that are true to the character and Biblical revelation. Many of these furnish profound insight into the nature of the gospel, the life of Jesus, and the way of human nature.

The questions with related Scriptures that follow each monologue focus the reader on the meaning of the story. Quite obviously this volume was not written merely to entertain or even to inspire. It was produced to bring about spiritual growth through a personal encounter with Jesus.

The uses for the book include many possibilities. An individual reading the volume will be blessed savoring the monologues in quiet privacy. A group Bible study will enable persons to share insights gained. Using the text as the basis for a monologue sermon or devotional will enable a class, a congregation, or a crowd (such as for an Easter sunrise service) to relive the reality of Jesus' presence.

This is a book I look forward to sharing with others. Those seeking to know more about Jesus will find here a means to make him real and not some shadowy figure from the past. Those who have followed Jesus for years will discover new insights concerning him and their relationship to him. Those who have just recently come to faith in Christ will discover a form of Bible study that will transform the personalities of the Bible into companions in their walk with Jesus.

William Tinsley through the years has proved that he is an extraordinary strategic planner and administrator. Here he displays a marvelous gift for communication. With a host of others I say, "Thank you, William Tinsley, for a fresh and inspiring look at the personalities who made possible the old, old story of Jesus and his love!" I look forward to the other volumes that I trust will follow in the same vein.

WILLIAM M. PINSON JR.
Executive Director Emeritus
Baptist General Convention of Texas

PREFACE

THE IDEA OF WRITING THESE STORIES WAS BORN OUT OF MY EXPErience on Good Friday, 1999. Two-thirds of the small community of Floodwood, Minnesota, had packed the school gymnasium for the Good Friday observance where I was scheduled to speak. Those present included members from the Catholic, Lutheran, Assemblies, and Baptist churches along with their priests and ministers. I told the simple story of Barabbas from his perspective with the obvious implication that Jesus died in his place, and drew the application that, in a way, we are all Barabbas. I was deeply moved by the responses of those present. It seemed as if they were hearing the story for the first time.

On Easter morning I told the story of Mary Magdalene to a congregation in Minneapolis with a similar response. It occurred to me that a growing number of people are hungry to hear the stories of those who met Jesus two thousand years ago as they might tell it. So I began writing. The result is the stories you will find in this book.

I have intentionally decided not to include the better known figures of Christian history: Peter, John, and the other members of Jesus' twelve, Mary the mother of Jesus, or Paul. Instead I have sought to develop the lesser known individuals who are referenced in the Gospels in order to gain a fresh look at who Jesus is and what it means to meet him personally.

The stories are written so they can be read as personal devotions. The scripture references for each story are included at the beginning so the reader can easily reference the accounts from which the story is constructed. After each story, I have included Questions for Reflection followed by Scripture references related to each question. Some may choose to use the stories as a catalyst for thought in small groups, using the questions and Scripture references for discussion and study. The stories necessarily include some assumptions such as the age of James the brother in relation to Jesus as well as the ages of Mary, Martha, and Lazarus in reference to each other. While the Bible is silent on this information, the assumptions are well within the realm of reason. In no instance have I included assumptions that would be contradictory to the implications of the Biblical account.

I hope these stories will help those who are exploring the Christian faith to better understand the individuals who were part of the first century experience and that all who read these stories will be moved to a deeper understanding of Jesus in their own personal faith in him.

JOSEPH

Matthew 1:16–25; 2:13–23
Mark 6:3
Luke 1:27; 2:1–51; 3:23
John 1:45; 6:42

I GREW UP IN AN OBSCURE VILLAGE IN GALILEE NAMED NAZARETH as a carpenter by trade. There was nothing about Nazareth that would attract others to it. Our village was tucked back into the cup of the hills, obscured from public view. But from the top of the hill above us could be seen a panorama of Israel's history. To the east lay the Jordan Valley, to the south, the vast plain of Esdraelon where Israel fought dozens of battles near the mounds of Beth Shan, Tabor, Gilboa, and Megiddo, and to the west rose the Carmel ridge that plunged into the Mediterranean. Military roads and trade routes could be seen not far away. But they all bypassed Nazareth. We were a village off the beaten path with little economic significance. Our town was widely reputed to be a haven for lazy and dishonest castaways. But it was our home. It was where Mary and I grew up and fell in love among the gnarled olive trees.

I had the ambitions of most young men: to marry, have children, provide for them with the work of my hands, and grow old enjoying grandchildren and family. Mary shared my dreams. We talked often about our future, about the home we would establish, and about the children we would raise.

Those were happy days when Mary and I climbed the cliffs above our village to the summit of the ridge. We could see the vast display of valley and mountains to the east, south, and west. We felt as if we sat on top of the world, young adults with our whole lives before us. We felt our hearts knit together in our engagement as strongly as any couple who have taken the vows of marriage.

I was crushed when I discovered Mary's pregnancy. She tried to explain it to me. She said an angel had appeared to her and she vowed she had been faithful to me. But I could not accept it. How could any man accept so fantastic a tale? I thought at the time she would have shown more respect if she would have simply been truthful about her tryst with someone else. It was not, after all, uncommon in Nazareth. The morals of our town were nothing to brag about.

I could have had her stoned to death for breaking our vows of betrothal. That was my right. Of course such action would have vindicated me in the eyes of my peers. No one would have blamed me. But I loved Mary. I could not think of hurting her even though she had destroyed all my dreams and shattered my confidence in the one person I loved. I decided to break the engagement privately. It was the only thing I could do.

That is when God intervened. I admit what happened to me was unusual. But those were unusual days, special days, never to be repeated. I guess God had to do something dramatic to get my attention. The same angel Mary had described to me appeared in my dreams and spoke clearly to me, telling me I was wrong. The child she carried indeed was not my child, but neither was it any other man's. This child was unique, conceived by the Spirit of God for a special purpose in God's plan.

Some would dismiss my dream as wishful thinking, an aberration of the subconscious. But I knew better. I knew this was not a normal dream. This was God speaking, and I must obey the inner compulsion of God, even if it went against all rational explanation.

The months went by and Mary's parents sent her away shortly after her condition was known. I hated to see her go, but it would be easier for her to spend her pregnancy removed from the gossip of those we thought to be our friends. She went to a village in the Judean hills near Jerusalem, to the home of her mother's cousin, Elizabeth. I busied myself with my carpentry, saving every penny I earned in order to provide for Mary and our family.

The visit with Elizabeth was good for Mary. When she returned she was aglow. Her understanding of what God was doing in our day had expanded in her talks with Elizabeth. She grew more sure, more confident, more excited (and larger) with each passing day. I grew more concerned.

Her belly was already swelling with the child when we married. Others talked. They assumed we had been indiscreet in our relations during engagement, that the child was mine, and that I had made her pregnant prior to sealing the vows in formal marriage. I knew there was no reasoning with them. After all, this was not a reasonable thing. If I had been in their place, I would likely have thought the same. It was a stigma we both would have to bear, a stigma our child would grow up with. I was learning a keen lesson regarding faithfulness to God, that often being obedient to his will results in being misunderstood by others, especially by the most pious and the most religious.

You can imagine my consternation when we received the summons for the Roman census. Mary was in her ninth month and we were required to return to the village of our ancestry to register for a universal tax. Never before had this been done. The timing could not have been worse for us. Since I traced my ancestry back to David, I was required to return with my wife to the city of Bethlehem, five miles beyond Jerusalem, ninety miles south of Nazareth. The thought of Mary making such a trip in her condition seemed impossible. But she did not complain.

We gathered our few belongings and set out, along with the others from Nazareth who were of the same family line. Mary rode upon a donkey most of the way. Occasionally she walked. I am sure the jostling upon the animal was uncomfortable for her. Frequently she grimaced and gripped her abdomen in pain, but she kept insisting she was all right. At night, when we camped and rested for the following day's journey, she would place my hand on her stomach to feel the movement of the baby in her womb. It brought her great pleasure to feel the baby, and even more for me to feel him squirming inside her. To be honest, it frightened me a little. What does a carpenter know about babies? Who was going to deliver this child, and how would we care for him once he was born?

We were familiar with the trip to Jerusalem. We had made it many times to celebrate the Passover in the spring of each year. We looked forward to familiar stops where we traditionally camped and rested. We marked our progress with familiar boulders and twisted trees that we had passed on the journeys of previous years. Once we reached Jerusalem, however, we were on unfamiliar ground. I had never visited Bethlehem. Like others, I knew its history: the home of Ruth and Boaz, the anointing of King David by the prophet Samuel, the return of Jewish exiles to this city from Babylon. I felt an exhilarating surge of adrenaline as we came in sight of the city. Something stirred within me that seemed to connect with the ancient history of my lineage, realizing my very existence sprang from the loins of David, King of Israel. For a moment, I forgot the pressures and worries I carried as I entered the town.

Bethlehem was teeming with energy. People had come from distant villages scattered across Judea and Galilee. Their accents were distinct, like my own, betraying in a single syllable the regional origin from which they had returned to register in the Roman census. The streets were packed with people. I had to shoulder my way through the crowd, asking for directions to the nearest place where we might find lodging. Most ignored me, too intent on their own errands to help a displaced foreigner from Nazareth. One motioned and offered directions to an inn that might house us. I gripped the rope of the donkey firmly in my right hand and pulled him grudgingly between the pressing crowd with Mary balanced upon his back. I shoved my way in the direction of the lodge, hoping to find a simple room where Mary could rest and we could both find respite from the thundering din of humanity.

I found the inn and excitedly rapped upon the innkeeper's door. He did not respond. I knocked again. Finally the door swung open revealing a short fat man with greasy hair. He looked up at me from the shadows of the half-open door, a scowl on his face, obviously irritated at my disturbance. I offered him money for a room, but he laughed. Bethlehem, he said, was packed. Every room of every inn in the town was taken. My money would do me no good. There was no place for us to stay.

I found this hard to believe. For months I had saved in order to provide for Mary and the child. And now, all my efforts were worthless. Mary's conviction regarding the special nature of this child's birth had grown with each passing week. But my own faith wavered. If this was really of God, then why were we having such difficulty? Could God not provide a simple place for us to stay?

A kind woman overheard me pleading with the innkeeper. As he slammed the door shut she introduced herself. Apparently she had seen Mary in her pregnant condition and felt some compassion for our plight. She told me of a place not far away, a stable for animals. "It isn't much," she said, "but it will give you shelter and a place to rest."

I gladly accepted and followed her to the stable. She wouldn't accept any money. She said God told her to help us. *If God had created this child and spoken to me,* I thought, *why should I question that God had directed her to do this?* I made a bed for Mary from clean straw and we settled in for the night.

After Mary slipped into a deep sleep, I stepped outside. The stars were unusually brilliant, sparkling in their positions against a deep blue. I had watched the stars often outside our home in Nazareth. Long nights I spent watching them slowly rise in the east in their familiar patterns, gradually rotating across the sky and disappearing in the west.

These were the same stars my ancestor David watched when he shepherded on the hillsides outside this city, the same stars Moses had seen when he wandered the Sinai. The stars have a way of crossing great generational gaps, uniting all mankind in a moment in time.

But this night there was a unique star, a brilliant star shining overhead, a star that did not rotate with the motion of the rest. I watched it for a long time before retiring to the stable where Mary was in a deep sleep.

It was still dark when Mary woke me. The labor pains were increasingly frequent. For hours she had suffered them in silence, letting me sleep, until she was sure the time had come. There was no holding back, no retreating. The baby would be born and life as we knew it would never be the same.

I had never been present at the birth of a baby. It was the custom for men to remain outside while the midwives helped the mothers deliver their children. But we had no midwife. It was just Mary and me. The pains came upon her more frequently with greater intensity. Even now, I am not sure how we got through the birth of our son. I have to give the credit to Mary. She is a remarkable woman. I have never known anyone with such courage and strength. Between the pains that took her breath away, she gave me instruction. She had watched many times and assisted her mother in the birth of other children. So, remarkably, she told me what to do, and I simply did what she said.

He was a beautiful boy with a lusty cry for life when he first was born. I bathed him and wrapped him in the clean cloth blankets Mary had packed for our journey, then cradled him in Mary's arms, and we slept. For the first time, I called his name, the name I had been given in my dream—Jesus.

We spent several days in that stable, Mary recovering and the baby gaining strength from his mother's milk. Strange visitors came to our obscure little cave, telling of remarkable phenomena that affirmed the unusual nature of the child we now nurtured. But I became increasingly disturbed. I could not sleep. Every time I closed my eyes for rest, I found myself writhing and wrestling with dark forebodings. It was a warning. I was sure of it. The child was in danger. If these strangers from such disconnected places knew of his birth, others would know, and I must hide him. There was only one place to go: southward, out of Judea, to a foreign place where no one would know us, to Egypt.

But first, we must fulfill our obligations under the Judaic law. So as soon as Mary was able to travel, we returned briefly to Jerusalem to offer sacrifice to the Lord God for the gift of this child. We were poor, like so many others. We could only afford a pair of young pigeons. But again, we were surprised and encouraged by those who did not know us.

When we walked into the courtyard an old man met us. He said his name was Simeon. It was not unusual for others to take interest in a newborn baby. We smiled kindly and agreed to let him see our child. But the look on his face was different. He did not look on our son like others who babbled the incoherent gibberish that adults always speak to infants. He gazed intently, his eyes filling with tears. He asked us if he could hold him, and we nervously agreed.

He held Jesus close to him, examining him like a jeweler examining a rare diamond and tenderly caressing him. Then he lifted our son above his head and began speaking words of praise and adoration to God. He said he had lived a long time waiting for this moment and that God's promise to him was finally fulfilled. He said he had now seen the salvation of Israel. His face radiated with a radiance I have rarely seen in my life.

He gently returned him to Mary's arms. Then, it was as if a cloud swept over his face. His expression became troubled and dark as he looked intently into Mary's eyes. He slowly spoke the words that neither of us have ever been able to forget. "This child is destined for the fall and rising of many in Israel, and for a sign which shall be spoke against. Be warned," he said, "a sword shall pierce through your own soul also."

He disappeared into the crowd and left us standing where we were, dumbfounded. We looked at our sweet child, resting so contentedly in Mary's arms, and at each other, wondering what kind of omen this could possibly hold for the future.

Hardly had the old man left before an even older

woman appeared. I don't know if Simeon had spoken to her regarding our child, or if she came on her own. But like Simeon, she studied Jesus intently, then burst out with praise to God for his birth. Her name was Anna. Others told us she had been a widow for eighty-four years and stayed in the temple night and day, fasting and praying in hope of seeing the Messiah of Israel. That day, you would have thought she was a youth by the boundless energy with which she spoke concerning our son.

After completing our sacrifice I wasted no time in leaving for our southward destination. The attention we were drawing made me even more convinced my premonitions were correct and that his safety depended upon our taking him far from Herod's control.

Egypt was good for us. We did not speak the language, but it was such a cosmopolitan center that we had little difficulty in finding someone who could translate and help us establish our little home. Fortunately, the need for a carpenter is universal, and it did not take long for my business to prosper. We stayed in Egypt for almost eight years, until we heard that Herod had died.

We determined it was finally safe to return to our home, but we carefully avoided the region of Judea where Archelaus was ruling in place of his father. I was fairly confident that enough time had elapsed that the Romans would have forgotten about the signs surrounding our son's birth, but I did not want to take any chances. So we quietly slipped northward into Galilee and returned to the obscure little village of our childhood—Nazareth.

Mary and I both knew I was not the natural father of Jesus. But I doubt if any father ever loved a son more than I loved him. He became my joy as I watched him grow. How he absorbed everything! Whatever he saw, whatever he heard, whatever he read remained complete and whole in his mind with instant recall. Others liked him and were drawn to him. No child has ever been so winsome as he. His spiritual discernment deepened far beyond my own, and I watched with pride and pleasure as his shoulders broadened, his arms strengthened, and he grew tall. We talked for hours into the night, sometimes all night. We communed together in the shop, working side by side in silence. He was, as I knew from the beginning, God's gift.

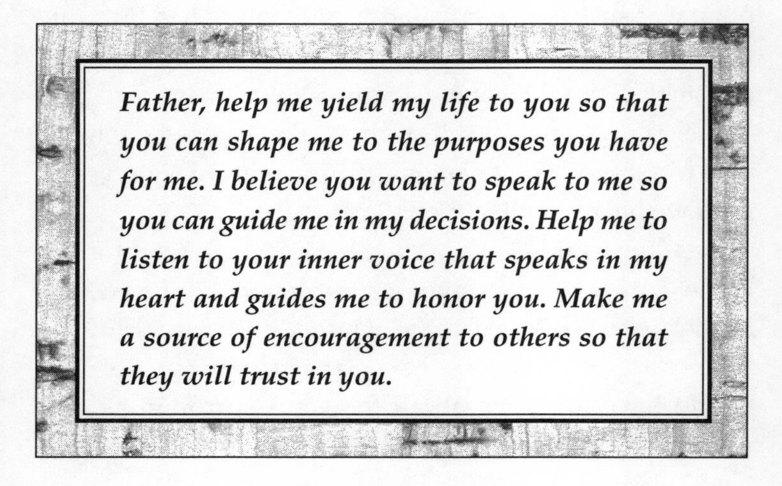

QUESTIONS FOR REFLECTION

1. Joseph's plans for marriage and a simple life in Nazareth were interrupted by the birth of Jesus. How do you respond to the interruptions that are beyond your control: the birth of a baby, the death of a loved one, the loss of a job?

2. God spoke to Joseph instructing him to accept Mary and protect Jesus by going to Egypt. How do you listen to God so he can lead you in your decisions? How does God make his will known to you?

3. Joseph and Mary found assurance and encouragement from Simeon and Anna. Who is God using in your life to encourage you in your faith? How are you encouraging others?

Matthew 13:55
John 19:25

I GREW UP AS THE YOUNGER SISTER OF MARY, THE MOTHER OF Jesus. My memories of our childhood are vivid, even today. We played as girls among the olive trees and vines that grew green on the hillsides. We watched with wonder as the pomegranates grew into huge pods that hung heavy on their branches, pregnant with their sweet seeds hid beneath red and orange skins. How we enjoyed breaking them open and sucking the sweet juice from the wet red seeds! We giggled and laughed in the joy of simple tastes and pleasures.

The well on the edge of town was one of our favorite places. The women gathered at the well daily to fill their pots with water for washing and cooking while the children played. The well was a social gathering place where our mothers learned of the latest news: who was engaged to whom, the latest births, deaths, and illnesses. We raced to the well with other children, our bare feet flying in the dust, our skirts whipping in the wind. Mary always won. She was the fastest. I don't remember anyone outrunning her to the well. How we laughed and how our mothers scolded us to be better behaved.

Mary's dark eyes sparkled with energy, sometimes a hint of mischief, occasionally a flash of anger, but always, not far beneath the surface, a bubbling joy. Her smile could light up a room. Everyone loved Mary, and Mary loved everyone. She knew the poorest beggars by name, stopping to visit with them, treating them with as much respect as one might give the mayor of our city. Mother often reprimanded her, warning her that she should not associate with the diseased riffraff that lay in the streets begging for alms. Of course, Mary had no alms to give them. But she did bring them fruit from the orchard, an occasional fig and plum to brighten their day. To look at their faces, you would think she had given them a week's wages. They smiled and beamed whenever Mary came near. Her joy was contagious.

Mary was a tomboy: climbing trees and sometimes, to the dismay of our parents, actually competing with the boys in their games. She was a natural athlete. Had she been a man, she would have been the strongest and swiftest in our city. As a girl, she didn't do too badly. Nothing was more infuriating to Mary than discovering the boys were making allowances for her. She wanted equal footing with them all, and believed she could win, whatever the odds.

Mary had a deep spiritual side to her. Sometimes she spoke of voices, of visions. But she learned not to speak of these things often. Others ridiculed and shamed her for pretending to have direct communication with God. Only the high priest could come close to God, and that only once a year in the Holy of Holies. Women were not allowed to speak or teach in the synagogue, only men could study the Torah. If Mother scolded Mary for her unconventional care of the poor, Father became outright angry when he learned of her assertions that the angels of God spoke to her. It was tantamount to sacrilege. So, understandably, Mary kept these things to herself. She only spoke to me on rare occasions regarding these mysterious messages. It scared me whenever she did. Perhaps it was because I was her sister, maybe it was something else, but when she spoke of these things, I knew she was telling the truth. I could tell she was frightened too. She never spoke of these things except in a whisper, and whenever she did, she always began to tremble like someone shaking with a chill from the winter wind. But her fear was overcome with her confidence that God was somehow choosing her, speaking to her about something special he had planned for her life. It was hard to understand.

From an early age, there was no one for Mary but Joseph. The rest of us thought it strange. They were so different: Mary so filled with adventure and Joseph so stable. When people thought of Mary they thought of her as energetic, enthusiastic, cheerful, competitive, inquisitive, unconventional. When they thought of Joseph, words came to mind like honest, strong, trustworthy, just, quiet, reserved, and dependable. But when they were together, their admiration for each other was obvious. Joseph could not help but smile when he watched Mary as she gathered crowds of admirers around her with her boundless joy. It was obvious that Mary adored Joseph. Mary and I stayed awake many nights, curled up in the darkness, whispering in our beds, giggling about Joseph, dreaming about the wedding and their marriage.

Mary and Joseph finally became engaged, legally bound together, but not yet married. Our families had agreed and all the arrangements had been made. Joseph, as would be expected, paid a handsome payment to our father, a fee known as the *mohar.* It was far beyond anything anyone would expect a carpenter to pay. But Joseph prized Mary, and he did not want to enter into marriage with her cheaply. Likewise, our father had already given Mary's dowry to Joseph as a pledge and a sign of commitment to their marriage. Both our families and all of our friends were thrilled about Mary and Joseph. The wedding was only a few months away, promising a full week of feasts and parties to celebrate the beginning of their new home. Everyone, especially those who gathered daily at the well, were buzzing about the wedding. But the wedding did not take place.

Mary told our family she was expecting a child. It seemed to me that she was completely surprised by the reaction. When she explained her circumstance to us, she did so with a trembling radiance that reflected awe rather than fear. She described a night visit from the angel Gabriel announcing the supernatural conception of the baby that was forming in her womb. But my parents only looked at each other in dumb disbelief. They had tried to tolerate Mary's fanciful imaginations of voices and spirits that spoke to her, hoping she would leave these things behind her as she matured. But now her attempt to explain her pregnancy in terms of a visit from God was too much. Who could blame them? When else has a child been born to a woman without having sex?

I have never seen my parents so mortified. Hardly a word was spoken in our home for days. The shame of it all was too painful for discussion. Father could not bear to look at Mary. He refused to even acknowledge she was in our home. He acted as if she did not exist. Mother only glanced at her, and that from the corner of her eye, a look that betrayed a combination of anger, reproof, and disappointment. Like Father, she did not speak.

Our parents decided to send her away to Mother's cousin, Elizabeth, far to the south of Galilee, beyond Samaria into the region of Judea. Elizabeth and Zechariah were the most respected religious couple in our family. Zechariah was one of the few who had the privilege of entering the temple as the priest of the people, to offer sacrifice to God in the Holy of Holies. Perhaps they could deal with Mary. Perhaps they could talk some sense into her head and dispel these wild imaginings about a virgin conception. Maybe something would happen. Perhaps she would lose the baby and all this could be hid from public knowledge.

If those were the things my parents hoped, they were not to be. Mary returned after three months more convinced than ever that this child was the result of a miraculous intervention of God. Everyone considered her delusional.

She was conspicuously pregnant and still betrothed to Joseph. No one suspected Joseph, of course. He was so strong, so honest and just, such a thing was unthinkable. But Mary! She had always been one to test the limits, to push beyond the borders. She had always been a child of deep passion for life. All the guilt and suspicion fell firmly upon her.

I remember the night of Mary's return when we gathered in our home for supper. We all ate in silence, our spoons slowly scraping the porridge from the bowls of pottery

Mother so faithfully set before us. Father ate little. He left his bowl more than half full and his bread still unbroken by its side. He rose without a word, put on his coat, and left. I learned later from Mother he had gone to return the gift, the *mohar,* to Joseph. The marriage was off. Mary's fate hung in the balance. She would likely be stoned for her obvious adultery.

I had seen one other person stoned to death, a harlot condemned by the elders. She was thrown into a pit surrounded by the men of our city who picked up stones and threw them. She tried to escape, clawing her way to the edge of the circle, but those who were there thrust her back and heaped heavier blows upon her with sharp, jagged rocks. One particularly large stone gashed the side of her head, knocking her to her knees. She cried and cursed, raising her hands in a feeble and futile defense. The stones rained furiously until every ounce of life was beaten from her body. It was an ugly sight. I could not bear to think of Mary being so brutally treated. But I knew the Scriptures required it. Deuteronomy 22:21 was clear and explicit and there was no bending in the law. Thankfully Joseph refused and decided to put her away privately.

We were surprised when Joseph came to claim Mary. His face was haggard with dark shadows beneath his eyes. It was obvious he had neither eaten nor slept for days. But his eyes gleamed with a glow that belied his emaciated condition. And when he looked at Mary, he almost worshiped her. He was tender and caring as he helped her gather her few belongings and took her with him. He said he must go to register for the tax to a small village south of Jerusalem named Bethlehem, and that he would care for Mary until after the child was born, after which he would receive her as his wife.

I think my mother and father were grateful. But they could think of nothing to say and remained heartbroken. From that day forward, they refused to mention her name.

What I remember most following that night was Mary's absence. She didn't return for a long time.

Word came that a baby boy had been born while they were in Bethlehem and that they had left for Egypt. Most assumed it was to escape the shame and the ridicule that she would have faced upon her return. At any rate, it wasn't until years later that she and Joseph came back to Nazareth, and by that time I had married and had a family of my own. Mother and Father died without ever seeing her again, or ever seeing the child she carried when she left.

I was thrilled when Mary came back to Nazareth. Sisters have a bond that cannot be explained. It was almost as if she had never gone away. But, then again, she was different. She was more serious, not as frivolous as she had been. She wept when she learned about our parents' death, sensing the disappointed and broken hearts they carried to their graves. But the joy was still there, a deep joy shared between her and Joseph that I have never seen between any other husband and wife. She was quieter, carrying, it seemed, a great weight within her soul. I asked her to explain her mystery to me, but she wouldn't. She would only smile knowingly with a sense of pity, and reassure me that someday everything would be made clear to everyone. I did not need to worry, she said.

She continued to care for the poor as she had when she was a girl. Only now she brought them baked bread from her own kitchen and an occasional coin from Joseph's meager earnings. The child continued to grow. What a lovely child he was. I have never known a sweeter child than Jesus. He had the same cheerful joy of life I had known in my sister, only deeper and more profound. People liked being around him and welcomed him into their homes. But there were those with long memories, who refused to forget, who seemed to find some odd pleasure in making sure Mary did not escape the illegitimate cloud that hung over her past. Mary ignored them, refusing to pay them any attention.

Mary and Joseph had other children, the boys, James, Joseph, Simon, and Judas, along with several daughters. They were a happy family, a busy one, with so many mouths to feed, and always, it seemed, a baby to care for. Mary seemed particularly concerned about Jesus. I thought it must be simply the fact he was the oldest. Parents always fret most over the oldest child, you know, worrying with each new stage of development whether they will successfully grow to maturity. By the time the younger ones come along, it is easier to relax, to know that "this too shall pass" and that, in the end, they will find their way.

But it was more than that. Mary had a foreboding about Jesus. She and her oldest son were particularly close, especially after Joseph died. Mary depended upon him to run the carpenter shop, to earn a living for the family, and to care for his younger siblings. I think she always knew he would leave because there was something he had to do, something she feared.

When he did leave, she was driven to distraction. He was thirty. Most of his younger brothers were already married and those who were not were old enough to take care of themselves. Reports began to come to us of his fame. It all seemed so strange, the stories so far-fetched. He never performed miracles when we watched him growing from childhood, but now they said he was healing the sick, cleansing lepers, causing the lame to walk, the dumb to speak, and the blind to see. We were in shock and disbelief that one from our village could possibly do such things.

He came back for a visit. The whole town turned out to see him, examining his face, his movements, trying to find some clue to the popularity he had found in regions beyond our little village. We gathered at the synagogue on the Sabbath and waited with baited breath to hear what he would say. Most hoped he would perform some miracle, display some magic. He sat down, received the scroll, and began reading from the book of Isaiah, a familiar passage everyone recognized as prophecy concerning the Messiah. And then, marvelous words, words we had never heard before, words filled with wisdom and insight into the Scripture we had never considered. The elders and the people alike were astounded.

But his speaking took a very negative turn. He began to speak about God healing Gentiles rather than Jews, choosing the pagan and unclean over the faithful descendants of Abraham. Their admiration quickly changed to rage. The smiles faded from their faces, replaced by frowns and glares of resentment. Suddenly, they remembered his beginnings, my sister's unwed pregnancy and her disappearance from Nazareth in his earliest years. They questioned his authority to make such blasphemous statements, the son of a carpenter, the illegitimate brother of my nieces and nephews who had married their sons and daughters.

They seized him and dragged him to the outskirts of the city, to one of the steep bluffs that overlooked the trade routes descending into the Esdraelon valley. They would have thrown him off the cliff, dashing his body to pieces on the rocks below, but he turned, gazed into their angry faces, stared directly into their disbelieving and accusing eyes, and walked through the middle of the crowd untouched. No one was able to lift a hand against him.

Mary began to follow him, along with a number of other women. And after awhile, I joined them. We had a growing confidence that he was indeed the special One sent from God. But none of us were prepared for the day he died.

I was there with Mary the wife of Clopas, Salome the mother of James and John, Mary Magdalene, the young woman who befriended him in his final weeks, and, of course, my sister. It was the Passover and we were all in Jerusalem observing the holy feast when suddenly news came that he had been secretly arrested, that a makeshift trial had taken place in the predawn hours, and that he had been sent to Pilate. The tragedy of the moment collapsed upon us without warning. We stood aghast outside the city, in shock as we watched him tortured. John, Salome's youngest son, stood with Mary close to the foot of the cross where he hung. I saw him speak to them with obvious agony, gasping for breath to form the words, entrusting my widowed sister to the care of his beloved young follower. I understood, for the first time, the reason for Mary's dark foreboding regarding her firstborn son. Only a mother can understand the pain Mary felt watching her son brutally executed.

We held each other that night, Mary and I, and we wept for long hours. It is a strange thing how an entire lifetime can be captured in the mind all at once, as if the beginning and the end are seen simultaneously with all the intervening time bound up in a single moment. That is how it seemed when he died. From the first day till the last, the visions of his face as a small child, the handsome youth, and the bold charismatic young man he became, they were all spun together like colors blending in a kaleidoscopic swirl of memory, washed with tears.

But Mary had a premonition. She sensed that all was not lost, that somehow God would intervene to justify the life she had carried, nurtured, and loved. I don't mean to say that she knew he would rise from the dead. I don't think anyone could have possibly expected something so shocking. Yet, her remarkable faith would not let her give up hope that God had some means by which this miraculous life would not have died in vain.

It was on the first day of the week that he appeared, and repeatedly afterward for more than a month, on many occasions, he was seen. The thought is still overwhelmingly awesome, to think that God chose us, an insignificant peasant family in a nondescript village off the beaten path, to enter into human existence so that we might know him. I guess in a way it makes sense that he would choose such an ordinary family and such an ordinary place. After all, God sent his Son for ordinary people.

We are now old women, Mary and I. The smooth skin and agile frames of our youth have long been replaced by the wrinkled brows, slumped shoulders, and bowed backs of old age. The beautiful black hair we once combed and braided so carefully has grown gray. But when I look into Mary's face, I still see the sparkling black eyes I knew when we were children. People still come seeking Mary, wanting to see her, to touch her, to hear her tell what he was like. She just smiles, like she smiled so many times with the beggars in the streets.

Dear Father, sometimes I think others do not understand our relationship. They have difficulty accepting my devotion and love for you. Help me to be understanding and patient with them as I wish them to be toward me. Thank you that you have loved me and made me feel special in your sight. Give me an unselfish love for others so that I can let them be who you want them to be rather than trying to make them into what I desire.

QUESTIONS FOR REFLECTION

1. The Bible tells us the people of Nazareth would have stoned Mary if Joseph had not interceded for her. They did not understand what God was doing in her life. How do you respond to family and friends who do not understand your faith in Christ?

2. Mary and Joseph were common people living in an obscure ordinary village, but because they were faithful, God used them to bless all generations. Even if your life is rather common and ordinary, in what way does God want you to trust him so you can be a blessing to others?

3. Mary had to let go of Jesus so he could fulfill his mission on earth. Sometimes the most difficult part of loving someone is letting them grow up and letting them go. When have you had to let go of someone you love? How did God help you?

Matthew 12:46–50
Luke 2:39–52
John 7:5
Acts 15:13–21
1 Corinthians 15:7
Galatians 1:19
James 1–5

OUR HOME WAS A HAPPY ONE. I REMEMBER MOTHER SINGING AT night, my father playing with us on the floor, laughing. And I remember my brother Jesus singing and laughing as well. From my earliest recollections he was there, four years older than I.

I treasured being with him. I idolized him, followed him as younger brothers will do, wanting to be included in his circle of friends, to be a part of older boys' games. He included me, defended me when I needed it, and looked out for me. Being with him was always an adventure. He found wonder wherever we went, whether it was wandering in the hills outside Nazareth; exploring rivers, ravines, and caves; or making up games with other children. He made everything fun. He saw miracles in the smallest things: ants building underground homes, a caterpillar spinning its cocoon, sparrows diving and looping as they chased huge crows from their nests, eagles soaring in the wind.

Our parents treated us equally. They loved us all the same. They never let on that he was different from the rest of us. I had no reason to think he was unique, other than the fact that he was my brother.

I was eight when things began to change. Jesus was twelve. We made our annual visit to Jerusalem for the Passover. Our family always looked forward to the date. It was a journey of celebration: traveling with family and friends; gathering in the Holy City with cousins, aunts, and uncles whom we had not seen for a year; listening to adults commenting about how each of us had grown, how much we looked like one of our relatives, how strong and handsome we were becoming.

Jesus seemed pensive on that trip, withdrawn and occupied. Not at all like himself, I thought. Then when we started home, after we had traveled a full day toward Nazareth, we realized he was missing. I had never seen my mother and father worried or confused before. But they were worried and confused that night. The next morning we left our friends and family, who continued on their way while we retraced our steps back to Jerusalem. My mother and father did not speak much. They were unusually quiet as we returned. They tried not to worry us, tried to act as if nothing was wrong, but I could tell they were anxious. It was written on their faces and underscored by their silence.

When we reached the city, they left me and my younger brothers and sisters with our uncle and aunt while they searched for him. All day they were gone. When night fell, they returned, the despair and anxiety written more deeply on their faces. When we went to bed, I could hear Mother crying, and Father trying to reassure her. "We'll find him tomorrow," he said. "Don't worry." But I don't think it helped much.

They left early the next morning, and returned with Jesus by midafternoon. I had never seen Mother angry before. I don't think I have seen her angry like that since. She would hardly speak to Jesus. Her face was cold, her jaw clenched as she began gathering our things, preparing once again to leave. Father tried to ease the tension. But it was useless. Something had happened that I could not understand. They had always trusted him implicitly. Maybe it was for that reason that Mother seemed wounded and hurt.

I tried to stay out of the way. I think, in many ways, it was the worst day our family ever experienced.

Things were never quite the same after that. Mother seemed more distant. It was obvious she didn't understand Jesus anymore. He was quieter, spent more time alone, sometimes wandering off into the hills for hours at a time. He worked hard in my father's shop, patiently shaping the wood into exquisite pieces of furniture. My father was a good teacher, and Jesus was an excellent apprentice. A close bond grew between Jesus and my father. They sometimes talked late into the night. Father seemed to understand him better than anyone else, even better than Mother. I sometimes felt envious of their talks. I wished I could talk to Father like that. As the years passed, I worked alongside my brother, learning the trade from him as he had learned it from Father. But often, his mind was a thousand miles away. Though his hands moved, repetitiously smoothing the wood, sometimes caressing the grain, it seemed his thoughts were in another world.

Oh, he still laughed. There were bright flashes in his eyes as when we were younger. But there was a seriousness that had not been there before.

It was only a few years later that Father became ill. It happened suddenly. His body was racked with fever. Mother bathed him with cool towels trying to comfort him, but he shook with chills and grew weaker. He died in a matter of days.

Jesus became the head of our house. He was only a teenager, but he was the oldest and we all turned to him. The shop continued to do well. He became a master carpenter, and he taught the rest of us the things he had learned from Father. But he was better. He was a perfectionist. Nothing ever left his hands imperfect or blemished. People were willing to pay high prices for his woodwork, but he refused to hike the cost. He often worked for free.

Mother leaned on him. Depended on him. There was nothing, she thought, he couldn't do. No problem he couldn't solve. We all depended on him.

I was twenty-two when I married and left home. He stayed, helping raise the younger ones, taking care of Mother, running the shop. Three years later it returned, the same pensive demeanor I had seen when he was twelve. He began spending more time away from the shop, sometimes early in the morning before the sun rose, sometimes all night. Occasionally he was gone days at a time. The worried look returned to Mother's face.

Word came of a preacher near the Jordan, a man named John who was preaching about the Messiah. We all went to hear him preach. Mother said she knew him. She told us his parents were relatives of ours and that she had known his mother before he was born. She seemed uncomfortable. We did not stay long, but Jesus did. In fact, he never came home again. Well, he did visit once, after he was famous, but he wasn't really home, it was just a visit.

Our neighbors had been anxious to see Jesus again. We had never had a celebrity from our town before. Nazareth was not well regarded, a rather nondescript little place. But everyone was talking about him. The stories we heard bordered on the incredible. People were talking of miracles and of his teaching. It was hard to believe the one of whom they spoke was the same brother I had known all my life.

The visit did not turn out well. The city leaders didn't believe him. They knew our family too well, a simple hardworking blue-collar family that fashioned the furniture in their homes. I had married one of their daughters. My sisters had married their sons. We were one of them, and he was one of us. It was too fantastic to believe that he could possibly be the One for whom all Israel was looking, the One of whom the prophets spoke centuries before. After Jesus spoke in our synagogue, they attempted to kill him, but he escaped.

Mother was silent. She said nothing. But, again, she looked worried.

The stories continued to grow. My brothers and I sat down with Mother to discuss the matter. The whole thing was becoming an embarrassment to our family. People were talking. I decided something must be done. So I arranged for my brothers and my mother to accompany me, to seek him out. We found him teaching in a village. The crowds were enormous, standing shoulder to shoulder in the streets surrounding the home where he was meeting with his disciples. We shouldered our way through until we were near the door. We could not get in, so I told one of those at the door to tell Jesus we were waiting for him outside, that we wanted to speak to him. But he didn't come. He said these were his mother and brothers, these disciples and all those who did the will of God. It was hard to accept. I felt rejected and resentful. It was difficult to understand how he could be so cruel to Mother. Mother, though, accepted it. She seemed to know. She wanted to be near him, but no longer, it seemed, as his mother. She just wanted to be included among his followers. It seemed my whole world was turning upside down. Even Mother was crazy. Was I the only sane person left?

Of course, Jesus wasn't cruel at all. The problem was mine. I didn't believe. I couldn't understand who he was or what he was doing. He grew up among us, in our home, but he was not of us.

It was not until after his death that I understood. I guess it wasn't until after his death that anyone really understood, including his closest disciples. Mother stayed with his followers during that final year. She was there when he was killed, and his disciples cared for her, especially John.

There were rumors, wild stories about his being alive. I still didn't believe, not until I saw him. He came to me, alone. He showed me his wounds, sat with me, and explained all that had happened, opened the Scriptures to me. Only then did I understand. Only then did I believe. Sometimes, those who are closest to the miracle have the greatest difficulty believing. That's how it was with me.

He was my brother and I loved him from our childhood. That, I guess, is the miracle, that God would choose to send his own Son into the world through our family, that he would grow up like every other human being, and that, in the end, we would know he was "God with us." Miracles are never far away. But then, neither is God.

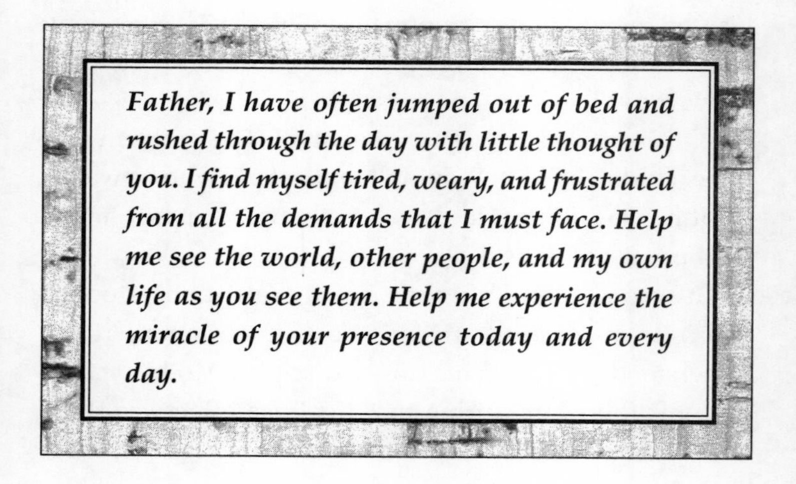

Father, I have often jumped out of bed and rushed through the day with little thought of you. I find myself tired, weary, and frustrated from all the demands that I must face. Help me see the world, other people, and my own life as you see them. Help me experience the miracle of your presence today and every day.

QUESTIONS FOR REFLECTION

1. Jesus often included references to the smallest and simplest aspects of nature to illustrate the beauty and presence of God: sparrows nesting in trees, flowers opening in multi-colored splendor, tiny seeds sprouting into huge trees. Take time today to reflect on the beauty and mystery of God's creation. Listen and look for evidence of God's presence in the world he has designed.

2. Where do you look for God? Do you only look for him in quiet and peaceful moments and in great cathedrals? God is present in the busiest and most secular moments of the day. When you are in the noise of the crowd, when you are in the workplace surrounded by others, think about God and look for him.

3. Have you ever experienced a miracle from God? How would you define a miracle? The greatest miracle of all is to experience the presence and goodness of God in ordinary and sometimes painful circumstances. Ask God to help you experience the miracle of his presence in your life.

ZACCHAEUS

Luke 10:30–37; 19:1–10

I WAS BORN AND RAISED IN THE ANCIENT CITY OF JERICHO, arguably the oldest city on the face of the earth, a city of tropical winters and steamy summers. Perhaps it was the hot climate, maybe the constant stream of strangers crossing the Jordan River who traveled through our city in search of trade, whatever the cause, Jericho was a restless city. Unlike the tranquil rural villages of Judea, Jericho was always bursting with energy, a crossroad of fortune seekers and pilgrims on their way to somewhere else. Jericho was never anyone's primary destination; it was only a way station, a place to stop, a place to buy and sell en route to other more pleasant places.

The anonymity of so many passing faces had an eroding effect on the value of human life. Strangers, a sea of strangers, that was Jericho. What did it matter to cheat a stranger? They would never be seen again, would never be missed. Maybe that is the reason thieves lurked in the passageways that led to and from our city.

It has its effect, this constant stream of humanity by which men become faceless forms in a passing crowd. It makes a man lose touch with his own worth, as well as that of others. That was certainly true of me.

I was short. When I was young, I was pushed to the side, ignored, despised for my small stature. Others grew tall, broad shouldered, and strong. But not me. I remained small, always looking up to others, both men and women, who towered over me in their full-grown height. But I was caught, stuck in a short body that failed to command respect or recognition.

When I was young I was taunted and ridiculed, rejected by my peers whose bodies blossomed and grew into the full bloom of womanhood and manhood. Often I stole away to my secret place, hidden in the shadows of the stone buildings, slipping away where I could not be found, so that I could weep in solitude. At first my tears were soft, tears of a broken and disappointed heart. I wept for myself. I wept alone. But the cold tears of grief turned hot and bitter, seasoned with burning salt. I wept tears of hatred and resentment. I wept until I could weep no more, until all the warmth within me was wept out and became cold, calculating, and cruel.

That is when I determined I would not allow myself to be overlooked, regardless of how short my stature. I might be small, but I was smart, and I would use my mind to overcome the gap that had grown between me and rest of the world. I decided to join the ranks of the tax gatherers.

Rome needed its taxes, and Jericho was one of the most lucrative sources of the wealth that embellished Pilate's palace. Everything was taxed: real estate, property, income, sales, and purchases levied with customs and duties. It was well known that the tax gatherers had the prerogative to increase the taxes, charging more than was due. Everyone took a cut, the collectors, the assessors, the soldiers, the government officials. It was a corrupt system from top to bottom. Everyone knew it. But no one could do anything about it. After all, Rome had the power. Anyone who resisted or refused the taxes levied by the collectors could be arrested and thrown into prison, or, even worse, struck down in the street by a sharp Roman blade.

Yes, I would become a despised tax collector, a Jew preying upon my own kind. I would amass a fortune from their misfortune and live a prominent, if despised, life of wealth. I had already felt the choking grip of rejection that suffocated my soul with isolation and loneliness. I might as well take advantage of the opportunity and be rejected for a cause. At least my wealth would create its own kind of friendship, the presence of those who liked money and those who had it. It was better than being poor.

The shoe was now on the other foot. Those who mistreated me I charged the higher price. Oh, yes, they grumbled and complained. I saw their clenched jaws and narrowed eyes peering at me sideways from beneath their furrowed brows. I heard their whispers behind my back. I'm not deaf. I heard them speak my name as if spitting it out in disgust: *Zacchaeus.* They pronounced it so that it sizzled hatred, drew it out so that it sounded like the hiss of a snake: *Zacchaeus.*

My father had given me the name. In Hebrew it means "pure." Ha! What a misnomer! Nothing about me felt pure. I had accumulated wealth, a fine home, rich robes, but within my heart, I felt the shame. When I closed my eyes at night I could smell the stench of my profession. I wasn't just hated by those I taxed. I hated myself.

That is when he came. That is when things changed.

As I said, Jericho was accustomed to a steady stream of strangers. But he was different. For two years he had been the topic of conversation. Everyone spoke of him, a prophet with miraculous powers. I had heard the stories of the lame leaping and running, of lepers whose skin became clean and whole when he touched them. They said he had fed five thousand men in the desert, manufacturing bread from thin air, that he had walked on the surface of the lake. And now, we heard, he had come to Jericho.

I have never seen the citizens of our city filled with such excitement. One who had been with him outran the procession and announced his arrival. He told us he saw him make a blind man see. His large eyes widened with wonder as he attempted to reenact the scene with exaggerated hand motions. He told how Jesus stopped along the way to help the poor blind beggar. I watched him recount the story. He replayed the blind man's desperate appeal, "Jesus! Son of David, have mercy on me!" Others tried to quiet him, he said, but Jesus heard the cry and ordered that the blind beggar be brought to him. The crowd grew still and quiet when the poor disheveled creature stood in front of Jesus. Everyone waited to see what he would do, to hear what he would say.

"What do you want me to do for you?" Jesus asked.

"Lord, I want to see," was the simple request.

Jesus responded, "Receive your sight, your faith has healed you."

Immediately the man who had been blind was able to see. He ran around feeling and touching faces he had felt before. But now, for the first time, he was able to see what he touched. He ran his eyes over everyone and everything, touching them with his eyes, it seemed, as he had once touched with his hands, drinking in the wonder of the newfound sense he had never known.

Crowds gathered around, catching the messenger's excitement. Like kindling brought close to the fire, they burst into flames themselves and told their friends as if they had been the one who had seen the miracle. Some gawked in amazement. Others shouted, slapping their knees. Friends embraced one another in celebration. Who wouldn't want to see Jesus?

People left their homes; vendors abandoned their wares in the marketplace. Everyone wanted to see the miracle worker from Nazareth. At first, I thought, I might as well join them. After all, there was little business to be done with everyone gone. But, the nearer he came, the more I felt myself swept up in the zeal of the crowd.

I couldn't see a thing: I was too short. No one would let me through to the front. They might do so for children, but not for me. They pressed together, pushing me further to the rear. Fathers hoisted their young upon their shoulders so they could see, but I was buried in the crowd. Everyone would see. Everyone would catch a glimpse. Everyone but me.

Then I spied the tree in the distance, a sycamore rising overhead, its limbs spreading across the avenue. If I could reach that tree before the procession, I would have an unobstructed view as he passed. I escaped the crowd and ran. My robes twisted about my legs, threatening to trip me, but I ran nevertheless. Breathless, I reached the tree far in advance of the crowd and began to climb. I know it must have looked strange, a grown man like me, clothed in my rich robes, shinnying up the side of a sycamore tree, but I didn't care. How I might have looked never entered my mind. I just knew I wanted to have a look for myself, to see this man who was unlike any other who had ever lived.

I perched in the fork of two limbs so I could securely watch him when he passed. I gripped the smooth surface of the sycamore bark firmly in one hand and propped my foot on another for stability. Fortunately, the huge leaves of the sycamore hid me from the eyes of the crowd. But an opening in the limbs gave me a clear view of the street. I could see him coming toward me in the distance, moving at the center of a crowd that almost mobbed him. His closest companions tried to protect him from the press. Yet, he seemed unperturbed. He did not mind. He moved like the eye of a storm, his white robe striking a contrast with the multicolored rags that raged around him. He came closer until I could see his face.

Then, he stopped! Just beneath where I was positioned. For a moment he looked about him, to each side, then he raised his eyes upward and looked squarely into my face. In that moment I wished I was anywhere else but there. I didn't intend to be seen. I didn't want to be singled out.

Every eye in the crowd followed his. The noise and din of the crowd quieted slowly, like an echo that slowly dies in a canyon. That is what it was like. I was suddenly in a canyon of time, an eternity, empty except for the two of us, Jesus and me. From the distant rim of the crowd a few cries still were heard, but around us, in that place, it was silent.

He spoke my name, "Zacchaeus."

He did not speak it as others spoke. There was no hiss of the serpent as he sounded the syllables. He did not spit my name in disgust as I had heard others speak, as if they were using my name as a form of profanity. When he spoke, the meaning for which the name was first chosen sifted through. He spoke it softly, gently, tenderly. Somewhere in the far recesses of my memory I knew it must have been the way my mother first spoke my name when I was laid in her arms after my birth.

"Zacchaeus," he said, "come down. I must stay at your house today."

How did he know me? How did he know my name? Why would he choose to spend the day with me, at my house? The shock of his statement almost shook me from the tree like an overripe apple ready to fall from its stem at the slightest breeze. I slipped and almost fell, but grabbed the limb and steadied myself instead.

The silence grew deeper. A gasp swept across the crowd followed by a murmur that sounded like water running over rocks. They were as shocked as I was, and not a little dismayed. Of all the people in Jericho, Jesus had singled me out, a tax gatherer, a known sinner, to spend his day with me, in my home.

I climbed downward as quickly as possible, then leaped the final few feet to the pavement, which was worn smooth by the constant shuffle of feet. I looked up into his face. He was tall, not the tallest man I had ever seen, probably a shade under six feet, but his stature towered over mine. He smiled.

I couldn't remember the last time I had seen such a smile. I had become accustomed to the frowns, the hard-set jaw, and clenched teeth of fellow citizens faced with the tax I levied upon them. What passed for smiles in my presence were sneers, scornful and derisive.

His smile was pure, perfectly unaffected. He smiled with his eyes.

I cannot express the thrill that swept over me. I was overcome with the honor and the privilege to have him spend the day at my house and enthusiastically led him through the streets to my home. The crowd continued to press him, but not as enthusiastically as they had a moment before. I could hear my name being whispered. I could see the consternation written on their faces. "Zacchaeus? He is going to the house of Zacchaeus, the tax collector?" They began to fall away the closer we came to my home.

I was proud of my home, one of the better houses in Jericho, built on a ridge with a magnificent view overlooking the city. I could sit in the terraced garden and see the ancient buildings sitting at my feet. I could see far in the distance the faded blue valley of the Jordan and mountains beyond. But somehow when he entered, my pride turned to shame. Suddenly I was overwhelmed with the realization that this house was nothing to be proud of. It had been purchased by dishonest gain, and I felt ashamed in his presence.

His companions joined him, the twelve who followed him wherever he went. I met Matthew, and learned that he, like me, had once been in the tax business. He told me of his encounter with the Master, how he had left his tax tables to follow him. He told me the things he had seen and heard.

That day all the loneliness I had felt, all the isolation, all the bitterness, resentment, and rage were washed away. A flood of goodness and compassion flowed from him like a river cleansing me and filling me with feelings I had never felt. I knew I was standing in the presence of God and he was accepting me, sinner as I was, willing to forgive me, inviting me into a new way of life.

After we had eaten I rose and stood before him. My eyes began to flood with tears. The colors of the room melted together into indistinguishable streams that refused to focus. I stammered as I spoke. "Lord," I said, "here and now I give half my possessions to the poor. And if I have cheated anyone at anything, I will repay him four times the amount."

I will never forget the words he spoke to me. "This day," he said, "salvation has come to this house."

Father, when I think about all the millions and billions of people on the earth, I find myself feeling small and insignificant. How could you possibly know me and care about my concerns? But you have demonstrated your love for me in your son, Jesus. Thank you for wanting to relate to me every moment of every day. Help me to give to others as you have so generously given to me. Forgive me of my selfish thoughts and fill my heart with generosity.

QUESTIONS FOR REFLECTION

1. In the overcrowded cities it is often possible to be in the middle of masses of people and feel unknown. Sometimes the presence of large crowds accentuates our sense of anonymity and loneliness. How do you handle your own feelings of loneliness and rejection?

2. Zacchaeus had no idea that Jesus knew who he was, and certainly did not expect Jesus to come to his home for dinner. God knows you. He knows everything about you. He wants to visit with you as a friend would visit at dinner. Talk to God as you would talk to a friend. Invite God into your home.

3. When Zacchaeus met Jesus, he changed from selfish consumption to generous giving. How does God want you to be more generous to others?

MARY OF BETHANY

Luke 10:38–42
John 11:1–44; 12:1–9

I LIVE WITH MY BROTHER AND SISTER IN A SMALL VILLAGE NAMED Bethany, about two miles outside Jerusalem near the Jordan River. Our parents died when we were young and my older sister, Martha, raised me and my brother. She was a teenager, seven years older than I, three years older than my brother. But you have to know my sister. If anyone could take charge of two younger siblings, it would be Martha. She is a very strong person. The neighbors wanted to split us up into different homes after our parents died, but Martha would hear nothing of it. She worked, from early in the morning until late at night, doing odd jobs to make ends meet in our simple home. She was as much a mother to me as she was a sister.

A few years ago huge crowds gathered near our home on the banks of the Jordan to hear a preacher named John. I slipped off, day after day, to listen to him preach. How he stirred the crowd! How he stirred me! Martha, of course, thought I was wasting my time. But I couldn't help myself. Thousands of people sat on the hillside to listen to John as he stood knee-deep in the gently flowing river. The multicolored clothes of the crowd decorated the hills like wildflowers. Their movement reminded me of a meadow bending and weaving in the wind.

When John spoke, they became silent and still, not wanting to miss a single word. He spoke with such boldness, with such courage and forcefulness. By the hundreds they responded to his preaching, moving forward to join him in the water, to be baptized by him as an expression of faith and repentance. He spoke with such conviction about the coming Messiah, about the end of the age, about the need to turn our hearts to God! My brother, Lazarus, was there when John pointed Jesus out.

We began hearing stories about Jesus' preaching, his teaching, and his healing. In a matter of months, his fame had spread throughout the region. When he returned near Bethany more than a year after John had pointed him out, Lazarus and I were determined to have him in our home. Martha was reluctant at first. But she gave in and opened our house to him and his followers. Of course, our home wasn't big enough for all of them. Some had to sleep outside, but they were accustomed to that. Martha was so anxious, cleaning and cooking, getting ready for their visit. We had never entertained so many people before, and certainly no one so well known. She wanted everything to be just right, spotless. Remember, my sister is a perfectionist.

I helped: swept, dusted, washed dishes. Lazarus gathered the list of groceries Martha instructed him to find: potatoes, onions, carrots, dates, cabbage, mutton. Martha had it all planned out. She knew exactly what we would cook, where everyone would sit, where they would sleep. But, when they arrived, all her plans went up in smoke.

They were a joyous group. I remember their laughter, fourteen men, my brother included, kidding one another as they enjoyed themselves. It was as if they didn't have a care in the world. Then the conversation changed. Jesus began to talk about spiritual things, the presence of God and his love. I had never heard anyone talk about God like that before, as if God were a person, as if we could know him intimately and personally, as if he already knew us. His words were magnetic, as was his voice.

The aroma of the supper drifted from the kitchen, the smell of vegetables and mutton mixed together in the air. I knew these men must be famished. They had walked many miles before arriving at our home that day, but they didn't seem to notice. They were all so intent on what he was saying.

I found myself drawn into their conversation. I sat in the circle with the men. They didn't seem to notice, but he did. He looked into my face in the same way he looked into the faces of the men. He let me know he was glad I stayed and listened. I couldn't take my eyes off of him. I was captured by every word that came from his lips, by the way he spoke, by what he said, by the beauty of his face and the love in his eyes. It was as if nothing else existed but that moment, as if I had been swept up in eternity. I never noticed Martha working in the kitchen alone, not until she burst through the door demanding I help her cook the meal. She asked Jesus to instruct me to leave.

I was embarrassed. I knew I was out of my place, that women belonged in the kitchen, that spiritual discussions were for the men, not for me. I am sure I blushed as I started to get up. I was personally mortified. But he raised his hand and motioned for me to remain. Then he told Martha I had made the right choice, that it was more important for me listen to what he had to say than to prepare the meal for them to eat.

I will never forget that moment. He handled it so kindly and so firmly. I remained and listened. Even Martha joined us and listened. We didn't eat for a long time. Food just didn't seem as important when he was around. Later his disciples helped us get the meal ready. They all pitched in to cook, set the table, serve, and clean up. Even Jesus helped.

That was the first of many visits he made to our home. But, when we thought we needed him most, he was nowhere to be found. My brother became sick. At first we thought it was simply a bad cold or the flu, but it worsened. No matter what we did, he lost strength. He wouldn't eat or drink. Martha and I knew his condition was serious. We knew that if Jesus would come, he could heal Lazarus as he had healed so many others. We were certain if he only knew that Lazarus was dying, he would stop whatever he was doing and come at once. We knew he loved Lazarus, just as we did.

We sent a messenger with a note to find him. Martha insisted on the wording: "He whom you love is sick." I guess we couldn't help sending a gentle reminder to him that Lazarus was special and that we expected him to come immediately.

He didn't come.

I couldn't understand it. Lazarus suffered terribly. But Jesus didn't come. My brother died. I heard the death rattle in his throat when he stopped breathing. I watched his fingernails turn purple then blue, like his lips, his face stone white. I watched them bury him in the tomb, and returned home with my sister to grieve. I have never felt so alone and abandoned in my life. I wondered how God could be so cruel. I wondered about the things Jesus had said about God and about his love. Did he really love us? If he did, why had he taken away our parents when I was a child? And why had he taken away my brother?

Four days passed. Then Jesus came. I was in the house with many of our friends who were trying their best to comfort me. In spite of their kind words, nothing helped the empty feeling I had inside. But Martha came over to me and whispered in my ear, "The Teacher is here, and he is asking for you."

When she told me this my heart leaped up to my throat. "Where is he?" I asked. She told me he was on the outskirts of the village, near the fig tree where the road turns toward Jerusalem.

I bolted from the room. I felt like someone thirsting to death in a desert who has just learned of an oasis that offers water. All I wanted was to be with him, to be near him. I felt that somehow he could assuage the pain that gripped my heart. I ran all the way to the place where Martha had left him.

When I saw him, I was overcome. The tears came again. I began weeping and fell at his feet. Through my sobs, I choked out the words, "Lord, if you had been here, my brother would not have died." I could tell he was deeply moved. I think he genuinely felt my sorrow, all of it, to the very depths. It was as if he breathed my sorrow into his own breast. For a long while he didn't say anything.

Then he spoke to those who were surrounding us, the crowd of friends who had followed me from the house. He asked them, "Where have you laid him?"

They offered to show him. "Come and see," they said.

I gathered myself and stood up. For the first time I looked into his face, and I distinctly remember the tears I saw forming in his eyes. Jesus was weeping. How could I have ever thought he didn't care? I knew in that moment that he truly loved my brother. In fact, he loved him far more than I could have ever imagined.

We walked together, following the crowd to the tomb where I had watched them bury Lazarus's body four days earlier. We stopped outside. Every eye was on him. No one dared to speak. His face began to change. His jaw was firm, almost clinched. His eyes stared directly into the tomb, staring, it seemed, straight through the stone that sealed its entrance.

"Remove the stone," he commanded. I heard the crowd gasp and murmur. It was such an incredulous command.

My sister stepped forward and reminded him, "But, Lord," she said, "by this time there is a bad odor, for he has been there four days."

Jesus slowly turned his eyes toward her. I had never seen his expression so serious, so commanding. He seemed to reprimand her, as if he were having some difficulty dealing with such trivial concerns. "Did I not tell you that if you believed you would see the glory of God?" he asked.

Martha immediately told our friends to do whatever Jesus commanded. Some of the men pressed their shoulders against the stone. They strained against its weight, but it slowly moved and rolled to the side, leaving a gaping dark hole where it had stood. I covered my mouth, partly out of fear, partly out of dread. I had no idea why Jesus was doing this. What could he possibly hope to gain by exposing the dead stench of our brother's rotting flesh. It seemed too much.

But I looked again at Jesus. His face seemed to glow as he lifted his eyes to heaven. "Father," he said, "I thank you that you have heard me. I knew that you always hear me, but I said this for the benefit of the people standing here, that they may believe that you sent me." I watched him. He was not merely looking into the sky. He was looking into the face of God.

Then he lowered his eyes, ever so slowly, and stared intently into the darkness of the tomb. His breath came more heavily, as if he were laboring. Then with a loud voice that resonated and echoed off the stones, he cried out my brother's name: "Lazarus! Come forth!"

We were all frozen for that moment in time. It seemed as if no one in the crowd even so much as drew a breath. I have never witnessed such silence, such intense suspense. I followed the gaze of his eyes, expectantly penetrating the dark opening, and then I saw the first faint shadow of something, someone moving within the tomb. Suddenly, from the blackness he stepped, my brother, alive from the dead! At first no one moved. We were all stunned. Then I stepped forward, moving slowly toward him, recognizing in the way he stood, the way he moved, the identity of my brother.

Jesus showed no surprise. He spoke softly so that only those who were close to him could hear: "Unbind the grave clothes and let him go," he said. Jesus seemed drained, as if enormous energy and power had gone out from him, leaving him exhausted.

The clothes still bore the stench of death. But inside those clothes, my brother was alive, more alive than ever before. He looked the same on the outside, but from that time on, Lazarus seemed to see things differently than anyone else, his perspective on this life and everything connected with it had changed. Sometimes he would sit for hours watching a small spider spin her web, its silver spans glistening in the golden gleams of the setting sun. Others would have felt guilty, as if they were wasting the hours of the day, but Lazarus seemed to have no concept of wasting any hours. He seemed to have no concept of mortality any more. We marveled at how he could live life in each moment without the slightest worry about the future.

Jesus stayed in our home the last week before he died. He left early every morning with his disciples, walking the two miles from Bethany to Jerusalem, and returned in the evening. Even in those final days when Jesus was with us, Lazarus seemed to know something no one else knew, not even his closest disciples. I remember late in the night, after dark, Jesus and my brother visiting, just the two of them. Jesus' disciples seemed worried. The carefree cheerfulness they exhibited when they first visited our home had disappeared. Their faces were long and drawn, tired and anxious. I overheard them talking about their fears, that something was about to happen, that the anger of the authorities in the Holy City was more intense, that some were plotting to kill him.

Even I felt it. I guess that is why I bathed his feet one evening with my own perfume. Something was foreboding. I could tell something terrible was about to happen. He understood why I did it. But his disciples didn't. Judas, the one called Iscariot, he looked at me with scorn and complained. "The perfume could have been sold," he said, "and given to the poor." Jesus reminded him the poor are always here, but he would not be.

I think Lazarus knew all along that death could not touch him, not ultimately, not finally. Now I know what my brother already knew, that this life is just the beginning for those who know him, that death is only a passage to a higher and greater life where our limited awareness is vastly expanded. The glimpse I had of eternal things when Jesus was near has taught me to experience every day as part of his presence and to look forward to a new world where my own grave clothes of this world will be discarded forever.

Father, forgive me for wasting my time, thinking I am busy about so many things, but finding my life a meaningless blur of activity at the end of the day. Help me to reflect on you at the beginning of the day. Help me remain conscious of your presence throughout the day. I know that you know what is best for me. Teach me more about your love and your life when you choose to answer my prayers differently than I expect. I love you, Lord. Let me live my life out of extravagant devotion to you.

QUESTIONS FOR REFLECTION

1. Martha almost missed visiting with Jesus because she was too busy when he came to her home. Reflect on the day you have just completed. What do you remember about the day? What kept you from reflecting on Jesus?

2. Martha and Mary appear distressed that Jesus did not immediately respond to their request for him to heal Lazarus. Reflect on a time when God did not do what you wanted him to do. What did you learn from the experience about God? About yourself?

3. The perfume that Mary used to bathe the feet of Jesus was very expensive, an extravagant gift expressing her devotion and love for him just before he was crucified. Do others see anything extravagant and costly in your devotion to Jesus? How do you express your devotion to him?

John 11:1–12:17

I LIVE IN THE VILLAGE OF BETHANY WITH MY TWO SISTERS, MARY and Martha. We are very close.

Our home is a quiet one, only two miles from the Holy City of Jersusalem, nestled on the eastern slope of the Mount of Olives, which separates our tiny village from the busy streets, crowded markets, and noisy temple of the city. Maybe that is why Jesus chose our home as his resting place whenever he visited Jerusalem. The commute to Jerusalem is not difficult. Anyone with average health can easily make the walk in less than an hour. Jesus and his disciples, walking with the quick pace of men who had walked hundreds of miles, could make the trip in less than thirty minutes, a pleasant journey in good weather.

As a youth, I enjoyed going to the summit of the Mount of Olives early in the morning at sunrise to sit, staring to the west, watching the City of David slowly shed the darkness of night and wake in the dawn with gray-shouldered shadows. As the sun crested the horizon to my back, its red-orange glow painted the landscape with crimson and gold, transforming the distant city into streets that seemed to flow with rivers of blood and light. The early morning silence slowly faded under the growing din of merchants and shopkeepers, shouting to one another as they sought the best bargains for their daily wares. By midmorning the city emitted a strange mixture of noises: the blend of animals bleating and braying, men shouting and cursing, priests chanting, people praying, and children crying and laughing. When I reflect on such scenes etched in my memory, I can easily understand why Jesus stood in this same spot and wept over Jerusalem.

As an adult, however, such occasions for reflection were few and far between. I was a carpenter, and a carpenter's day begins early and ends late. But I enjoyed my work. There is something satisfying about working with your hands, watching wood transform under the touch of your fingers into useful forms of furniture that will ornament a room with both beauty and usefulness. I felt, in those solitary hours of creativity, as if I were a partner with

God. The olive wood and oak, which God had created with his life-giving power, was now entrusted into my care. I simply released the beauty within, carving and shaping and polishing until the grain was drawn to the surface, exposing brilliant patterns unique to each one, like snowflakes falling from the sky.

Maybe that is why Jesus and I became such close friends. He was a carpenter as well. Mine was a simple carpenter shop with a well-worn bench and simple tools of my trade: the plane I used daily, its wooden handle and knob shining with the glow of constant use, various awls for puncturing and drilling holes of precise dimensions, saws with sharpened blades, and pieces of wood waiting to be worked. He seemed drawn to my shop. I think it reminded him of his childhood. He spoke little about the days of his youth, but I could tell he held fond memories of simpler times. He was, of course, a celebrity by the time I met him. But like most people who achieve fame, or for whom fame overtakes them, he seemed to miss the earlier days of anonymous solitude. My shop, I think, rekindled these feelings within him and gave him momentary rest from the growing weight of public pressure.

We spent many hours alone. His disciples rested and relaxed in the house and yard, visiting with each other while he and I slipped off to my place of work. The solitude seemed to strengthen him. Sometimes he spoke of his childhood, his days as a youth in Nazareth, working with his father. He knew the type of wood from its fragrance and its grain. He knew the trade well. He asked if he could help, and naturally I welcomed the offer. I watched him caressing the wood with its smooth grain, shaping and polishing the pieces that would become cabinets, chairs, and tables. He stroked the wood as lovingly as he stroked the face of a child, or as gently as he held the hand of a grieving widow. In such moments he disappeared into an inner world no one could penetrate. He was entirely alone at those moments—alone with his own thoughts, alone with God. He seemed to commune with God as his tender and strong hands continued to move. Occasionally, I thought I saw his lips moving, as if he were conversing with someone, talking with another who was present with him. I felt at such times that the Other presence with whom he was conversing was more real, more present, than even I.

We smiled knowing smiles. We laughed the laugh men laugh with pride when they finish a task. We spoke little. We didn't need to. There is a communication that does not require words between men who love the same trade. Besides, he spent his days dealing with words. He needed this quiet place and this comfortable activity to refresh and renew. I know it sounds strange for me to say it, but it was a profound spiritual experience, almost an act of worship, to work in my carpentry shop together. I guess that is what gave us such a unique bond, a friendship few others shared, including his disciples.

Of course, you want to know about the miracle. Everyone wants to know. Many of the scribes and Pharisees have visited our home since that day, always wanting to know, "Was it true, did I really die? Did he raise me from the dead? What did I see? What do I know?"

Yes, it is true. Everyone in Bethany knows the truth. After all, they saw my corpse. They buried me, wrapped my body in the linen cloths for burial, applying the death spices to offset the stench of my rotting flesh. They all knew, not just my sisters, but our friends as well. They saw and knew that I was dead.

It isn't hard to die, you know. We make such a big deal of it, as if it is difficult. But there is little pain, at least I felt none. Dying is a matter of letting go, of relaxing, resting. Of course I struggled at first in my illness, trying to get my breath, to throw off the fever, but then there came a calm, a quiet deep within my soul, and I knew it was time. Dying is not a matter of effort. It is like lying down on a floating barge and letting the current gently sweep you downstream to a destination over which you have no control.

What is that? What did I see? What was it like? I am sorry. I wish I could tell you. But there are no words. At first I tried to tell those who asked me, but I found it was useless. We have no language sufficient to communicate life beyond the grave. All the references here, all the words and expressions I might try to use, only trivialize the reality that resides beyond the breath of mortal man.

Imagine, if you will, if a man born blind asked you to describe the sunrise to him. What would you say? How would you describe the fading darkness, the dim glow on the eastern rim, the intensifying streaks of gold and crimson crossing the eastern sky, the reflections of rose-colored clouds rolling overhead to the west, followed by the burst of golden light growing in intensity until it blinds the human eye. Yes, you can understand the sunrise when I describe it because you have seen it. But a man born blind? How does he who has never seen understand? It is impossible.

That is what it is like for me to tell you about my experience beyond the grave. There are no words in the human language. There are no references, no likenesses. I am always attempting to describe the sunrise to men born blind. It is impossible.

I remember, though, the sound of his voice. It was distant, echoing faintly far away. He was calling my name, "Lazarus! Lazarus!" I felt myself moving toward him. It is a strange memory. I remember wanting to stay, to remain where I was, in that world beyond this one, but, more powerfully, I felt myself drawn to his voice. How could I resist? I can tell you this: Were it not for his voice, I would not be here. Nothing could have coaxed or commanded me to return to this world except that voice which called to me beyond the abyss. Only he could have called me and caused me to reenter this mortal form of dying flesh.

What is that you say? I look so much younger than my sisters? Ha! Yes, we get a good laugh out of that. Everyone says the same thing. I am actually three years younger than Martha, but four years older than Mary. But you think I look ten years younger than either of them? It's quite simple, really. Have you ever skinned your knee and had a scab form over the wound? When the scab falls off, what do you find? Yes, that's right, new skin, pink and fresh, younger than the old skin that surrounds it. That, of course, is a miracle too; we just expect it and take it for granted. Mine was more unique. But, when he called me out of the tomb, he restored my flesh, just like God restores your flesh when you skin your knee. That is why I look so much younger. But it is still flesh, and I will grow old and die.

My perspective has changed, however. I see people all around me trying to hold on to this life so desperately. I see those around me striving to accumulate wealth for this world, worried and exhausted, even selling out their very soul in dishonesty and deceit in order to get ahead, and they are so mistaken. It is the life to come that makes this life meaningful, even enjoyable. Now I see reflections of the eternal in the temporal. I find it in the bud of a flower, the buzz of a bee, the flight of a bird, the rising and setting of the sun. I see it in the face of a newborn baby, of a mother caring for her child, of a friend sacrificing himself for a friend, of a stranger helping another.

When you know your destiny in heaven, there is nothing anyone can do to harm you. You can suffer any injustice, any sorrow, any difficulty, because you know this world is only a phantom. The violence and injustice we see here will all pass away. Only those who succumb to the temptation of this world, to fight violence with violence, to defeat those who deceive by practicing deceit themselves, to cling to their possessions in hope of personal pleasure and security, these are the ones who die. Those who are able to see beyond this world, to perceive the permanent realities I have seen, to see as he saw, so that they live by a different "law," these are the ones who truly live.

Some people think I am crazy. They think my brain was starved for oxygen, that I suffered irreparable damage, that I am out of touch with reality since the day he called me from the tomb. But they don't know. I have never been more sane in my life.

I have met many who have been confused by what he said, about the meek inheriting the earth, about the merciful finding mercy, about those who mourn being comforted, about the poor in spirit inheriting the kingdom, and about those who are persecuted being blessed. They think his teaching is so foreign to the way the world really works. But when you see what I have seen, it all makes sense. I wish I could tell you. Then you would understand the reason he said what he said and did what he did.

He was not out of touch with reality. He was, of course, the only one who ever lived who was truly in touch with that which is truly real and eternal. I know!

AUTHOR'S NOTE: The Bible does not tell us what profession or trade Lazarus practiced. I have chosen to describe him as a carpenter in order to illustrate the close friendship that existed between him and Jesus.

Father, thank you for choosing me as your friend. This is an awesome thought, that the God of the universe would care to be my friend. Thank you for showing your friendship to me in Jesus. Thank you for a friendship that will last beyond the grave. You are my friend forever and I look forward to our friendship in heaven. Help me to live my life on this earth so that I will have no regrets when I see you in heaven. Help me to forgive others and love others as you have forgiven and loved me.

QUESTIONS FOR REFLECTION

1. The Bible tells us Lazarus was a "friend whom Jesus loved." Think of Jesus as your friend. Confide in him as you would confide in a friend. Talk with him as you would talk with a friend.

2. Do you think often of heaven and eternal life? How does your belief about heaven change the way you live today?

3. Think about your relationships to others, especially those close to you. Are you carrying any grudges or resentments or seeking revenge? How would Jesus respond to the those who have caused him to suffer?

Matthew 27:55–56, 60–61; 28:1
Mark 15:40–41, 46–47; 16:1–11
Luke 7:37–38; 8:1–3; 24:10
John 8:3–11; 19:25; 20:1–18

I WAS RAISED IN A FISHING VILLAGE NAMED MAGDALA ON THE northwest shore of the Sea of Galilee. Mine was not a happy childhood. I have tried to blot most of the memories from my mind, but still they haunt me, memories of abuse and neglect. For as long as I can remember I was an outcast.

I remember the religious people going to the synagogue, dressed and clean, ignoring me, looking down on me. I knew I wasn't good enough to be one of them. I knew they thought I was trash. So that was the way I acted, like trash. That was the way I thought about myself, as if I were trash.

When I became a teenager men noticed me. They didn't

look at me like the good and pious people who despised me. I know now the look I discovered in their eyes was neither love nor adoration. It was simply lust. But they wanted me, valued me in a way, until they satisfied their cravings. Then they walked away.

At first I gave myself to them because I found the only semblance of worth I had ever known. Now I know it was not even a cheap counterfeit of the real thing. As I grew older, I became desperate. I gave myself to men for money. It was the only way I could find to survive.

By the time I was in my mid-twenties, survival didn't seem worth it. My life was a waste. It wasn't worth living. I was depressed, despondent, hopeless. Almost daily I thought of suicide. I guess I would have taken my own life if I had not been such a coward. I hated myself even more for not having the courage to end it all.

I was a liar. I had learned to live on lies. I lied to others. I lied to myself. I lied so much, I think I got to the point I could not discern the truth from a lie. Sometimes I even convinced myself that my lies were true, which is not a hard thing to do when your whole life is a lie.

I was a thief. I had no qualms about stealing. Life had cheated me, why should I not cheat others? If they were stupid enough to leave things out where they could be taken, they deserved to be ripped off. So I stole from anyone and everyone. I decided life wasn't going to give me anything unless I took it.

At my lowest point, I was caught in the act of adultery. A bunch of religious men broke into the room where I was. They weren't interested in the guy. They were only interested in me. They grabbed me, half clothed, and dragged me into the street, kicking and screaming and cursing. They said I had seven devils and that I didn't deserve to live. They were going to stone me. Many of them held in their hands the stones they intended to hurl at me. I'm not sure I really cared, but I cursed them anyway.

They threw me in the dust, at the feet of a rabbi. I lay there, surrounded by those who were about to kill me, glaring at them. Then the rabbi began writing in the dust. I don't know what he wrote. I never learned to read. But it was something that surprised my tormentors. They murmured among themselves as he wrote.

Then he looked intently at each one of them, a look of such courage and confidence I had never seen. He challenged them, anyone who was without sin, to cast the first stone. The silence was deafening. Then I heard a stone drop to the ground, and another and another. They backed away, returning to their houses, or wherever they came from, until I was left alone with the rabbi.

He was different. He didn't look at me like other men looked at me. Neither did he look at me like the religious people I had known, even though he was obviously a respected teacher in the synagogues. He didn't despise me or reject me. Neither was there any lust. He looked deep within me, into the depths of my soul. I felt as others have felt who met him, that he knew everything I had ever done, everything I had ever thought, and he loved me still. I had never felt such compassion and acceptance. For the first time in my life, I felt I was a person of worth.

He asked where my accusers were. There were none. Neither would he condemn me. He told me to go and sin no more. For the first time in my life, I actually believed that was a possibility, that my life could be different.

He spoke of God and of his love. He spoke of his Father in heaven and his compassion for me. He didn't speak like the others who went to church. He spoke simply in stories and images I could understand. I hung on every word that came from his lips. He changed me. I did not need men anymore to prop up my poor self-esteem. I didn't hate myself. I felt deeply and truly that God loved me, and for the first time I loved myself. How could I express my love and gratitude to him?

I found him going into the home of one of the Pharisees. He was going to dinner. I knew I was not invited and that I should keep my distance from him. But I knew he would not turn me away. I slipped in while they were reclining at the table, gently unfastened his sandals from off his feet. I then opened my most precious possession, an alabaster jar of perfume, and began washing his feet. I couldn't help it. I was so overcome by my love and gratitude for what he had done that I began to weep. My tears fell like huge raindrops. I bathed his feet with my tears. I unloosed my hair from behind me and wiped his feet with the hair of my head.

The man in whose house he was visiting was incensed. He knew my reputation and scoffed at my action. It was obvious he despised Jesus for allowing me to do this. But Jesus defended me. He understood. He knew it was my overflowing gratitude to him that I could not contain.

Not long after this, they arrested him.

I was there, in the crowd, standing at the feet of our governor, Pontius Pilate. I watched and listened as Pilate addressed the crowd. He offered a choice. He would release Jesus to us if we wished. But those around me began chanting another name, calling for the release of Barabbas. I knew Barabbas. He was a notorious criminal, a murderer. He also liked women. Yes, I knew Barabbas. I could not believe my ears. These people, respectable people, were calling for Barabbas, a man who killed and used others, a man wrapped up in himself, a man who was brutal and cruel.

Then, to my horror, when Pilate asked what they wished him to do with Jesus, they began to chant, "Crucify! Crucify!" The chanting grew louder, more determined. Then Pilate washed his hands of the matter and sealed his fate. My heart was in my throat. This could not be happening! They couldn't crucify him!

After three hours of torture he was brought out again, broken, bruised, bleeding, barely able to stand to his feet.

The cross on which he was to be executed was loaded on his back and he was whipped, compelled to drag the huge weight through the street to the place of his death. But he was not strong enough. The beating by the soldiers had taken too much out of him. He stumbled and fell. He looked into our faces, a group of us women who were weeping for him. He spoke to us between short breaths. He told us not to weep for him but to weep for ourselves and our children. He said, "If they will do this when the tree is green, what will they do when the tree is dry?" I wasn't sure what he meant, but I have never forgotten what he said.

Another man was pulled from the crowd to carry his cross while he stumbled along behind. They took Jesus outside the city wall, and nailed him to the cross. I was there. I watched. I saw the nails piercing his feet. I saw him covered with blood. Again he spoke, "Father, forgive them, for they know not what they do."

About three in the afternoon, he died. He looked up to heaven and cried with a great voice, and his body went limp. He hung there for some time, until sunset was nearing. They broke the legs of the two who were executed beside him, but a soldier stepped up near the cross, drew his sword, and thrust it into his side, between the ribs, through his heart. Blood and water gushed out. I saw it. It was horrible.

About that time a very wealthy and religious Jew spoke to the soldiers and showed them a piece of paper. They nodded and took his body down from the cross. The man and his friends were hurrying because the sun was about to set, and according to their religion they could not work after dark. Some other women were watching and followed them as they took his body to a nearby cemetery. I went with them.

The Jew was named Joseph, Joseph of Arimathea. He was obviously grieved, like the rest of us. He was a wealthy man and he had a beautiful tomb carved out of the rock. It was to be his own burial place, but he wanted Jesus buried there. When his body had been placed in the tomb, several men heaved a huge boulder over the mouth of it so that it could not be opened. Then we left.

The women were kind to me. They had known Jesus too. They didn't care about my reputation. They accepted me and let me stay with them. They told me we would return after the Sabbath to finish the burial and place spices on his body. I was so grateful they were willing to include me. I would have gone immediately on the Sabbath. It didn't make any difference to me. I was never religious anyway. But they insisted we had to wait.

That was the longest day of my life. Most of the day I wept. I was not even aware of the sun rising or setting. The entire day seemed plunged in darkness. I remember people whispering, muttering things back and forth. I caught glimpses of Peter and some of the other disciples, but they kept looking over their shoulders. They seemed nervous and, for the most part, they remained elsewhere.

I couldn't sleep. What little sleep I got was fitful, full of nightmares, images of torture and death. Sunrise on Sunday could not come soon enough. Long before the sun rose, we were up, the rest of the women and I, preparing the spices we would use to complete his burial. The eastern sky was growing light, streaked with gray, slowly yielding to crimson, when we walked through the streets toward the cemetery. Along the way, the others began discussing the matter of the boulder. How would we get into the tomb? All of us together were not strong enough to remove the stone. We had no answer, but we hoped there would be a way.

When we arrived, the eastern sky was rimmed with gold, and, to our surprise, the tomb was open. The stone was standing to one side and a man clothed in a radiant garment was sitting upon it. I could not tell if the light radiated from the man himself or was simply a brilliant reflection of the sun bursting over the horizon. The others told me he was an angel. I guess they were right. He told us Jesus wasn't there, asked why we were seeking the living among the dead, and instructed us to tell his disciples. The others dropped their spices and immediately began running to the house where Peter and the rest were staying. I ran with them. I think we ran as much out of fear and confusion as anything. The disciples wouldn't believe us. I didn't know what to believe. I was so confused. I saw Peter and John whispering to each other in the corner of the room. I told them that his body had been stolen and we didn't know where they had taken it. Shortly afterward, they slipped out the side door. I followed them. I'm not sure why. I couldn't help it. I felt I had to follow. They started running. John was fastest and easily outran Peter. I ran as fast as I could. I was young and had always been a good runner, so I stayed close behind.

When we reached the tomb, John stopped outside and Peter passed him, rushing in. Then, a little later, John stooped in and disappeared along with Peter. They weren't inside long, a few moments, then they reemerged. Peter looked worried. His brow was wrinkled. He was so deeply engrossed in his thoughts that he did not notice me. John's face was glowing. He seemed elated. He brushed past me, hardly recognizing I was there. Then I went in.

The tomb was dark and empty. I saw the shelf on which we laid his body. His body was gone. The precious linen cloth that Joseph had wrapped him in was folded and lying to one side. I remember distinctly. It was a very expensive cloth of the best quality. I had examined it closely. But his body was not there. I could control myself no longer. I began to weep, not the gentle weeping of a few tears, I was sobbing uncontrollably.

I turned to exit the tomb, my tears blinding me as I tried to find the sides of the doorway with my hands but a man was standing in my way. I assumed he must be the gardener tending to the well-kept grounds of the cemetery.

He asked me why I was crying and who I was looking for. I pleaded with him to help me find the body of Jesus. I hoped, if he had taken the body, that he would show me where it was.

What I heard then I will never forget. He spoke my name, "Mary." I knew that voice. Though my tears were clouding my vision, my ears were clear. His voice was unmistakable. Once you heard his voice, you never could mistake it for another. No one called my name like he did. My tears continued. But they were no longer tears of grief and despair, they were tears of utter joy. I fell at his feet and locked my arms around him. How I loved those precious feet!

He told me to release him. He had not yet ascended to our Father. But he told me to tell his disciples, which I was overjoyed to do. Of course, they still did not believe, not until they saw him for themselves. Then we all knew that even death could not conquer him, nor will it ever conquer me. He has changed all that!

AUTHOR'S NOTE: The Bible does not identify the woman caught in adultery and dragged before Jesus in John 8. I have chosen to represent her as Mary Magdalene to illustrate her condition of having seven devils before she met Jesus.

Father, thank you that you free me from my past. The things I have done wrong, the injustices that I have experienced, you wash them all away and make me new. When the dark clouds of depression come, I pray that you will sweep them from my mind and help me to meditate upon your goodness and grace. You have more for me than I have ever imagined. Help me to see myself as you see me. Help me to see others as you see them. Forgive me when I prejudge people by their appearance and fail to see how much you love them.

QUESTIONS FOR REFLECTION

1. Do you have memories of neglect or abuse that haunt you? Memories of things you have done that you regret? Present these memories to God, one by one, and let him cleanse your mind and heart. He does not want you living your life wallowing in guilt, resentment, or regret.

2. Do you ever wrestle with depression? Talk with God about how you feel. God desires to give you hope. God's voice is always the voice of encouragement. He never discourages. He never desires for his children to despair.

3. Do you know someone like Mary Magdalene? How would you describe someone who has seven devils? What would they look like? How would you accept them if they came to your church?

Matthew 27:16–26
Mark 15:7–15
Luke 23:18–19
John 18:40

THE DARKNESS OF MY PRISON CELL DIMINISHED IN THE EARLY dawn. I had been awake for hours. In fact, I had not slept the entire night. How could I possibly sleep, knowing this was likely the last night of my life? Throughout the unlit hours I had plenty of time to think, to reflect on the events that brought me to this place.

I had been a leader from my youth. Whatever I did, others followed. Some say it is a gift. I don't know. As a child I pulled youthful pranks, the usual kind of nonsensical things that irritate adults. Then came petty theft. I was good. So were my friends.

It wasn't long before I graduated from petty childhood theft to armed robbery and insurrection. We stole from the Romans and the despised tax collectors to finance our operation. We struck when least expected, terrorist strikes that made the Roman establishment tremble.

I killed on more than one occasion. I was young and quick, able to strike an unsuspecting Roman soldier before he could defend himself. The first time I killed I felt a surge of power, as if all my rage and anger were suddenly focused like a hot beam of light burning in pinpoint concentration through a glass. I felt no remorse. I plunged the blade of my dagger into a man's abdomen, ripping and slicing his bowels. I saw the fear in his eyes, the terror on his face. I felt his hot blood drenching my hands. It dried in a sticky paste so that I had to pry my fingers loose from the dagger's grip.

They hunted me down—the Romans did—calling me a criminal. Maybe they were right. While others wasted their time praying and looking for a Messiah to free them from the Roman oppression, I offered action. I understood the world and its ways. Force must be met with force, terror with terror.

None of this mattered on that final morning when the rising sun lighted my cell. Nothing mattered any more. It was all over. I would be dead before dark. The Romans would make sure of that. They would make an example with my death and would enjoy every moment of the torture, dragging out my suffering as long as possible to inflict the maximum pain.

As the streams of light grew brighter through the barred window, I heard noise in the street. A mob had formed, or so it seemed, and Pilate was trying to appease them. Two other prisoners who had been captured along with me shared my cell. They also shared my fate. We would all be crucified together before sunset.

We listened intently to the crowd, wondering, hoping that by some twist of fate our destiny might be changed. The guard brought breakfast. But none of us could eat. How does a man eat when he knows he is about to die? I felt sick in the pit of my stomach.

The morning was dragging on. The mob grew restless outside. The streams of sunlight sifting through the dust-laden air slanted their shafts at steeper angles. Then the door groaned, creaking against its hinges as it opened. The guard snarled my name, "Barabbas." I stood, not wanting to expose my fear, wanting to appear defiant. He spoke no word, no explanation. He grabbed me by the shoulder and twisted me around, shackling my hands behind me, then shoved me through the door, out into the corridor. My shoulder crashed against the stone wall opposite my cell and I fell to the floor. I rose to my feet and tried to gather my bearings. I was in a long, dank hallway, dimly lit, littered with rotting bits of food, slop that had been fed to the prisoners days before, thrown in protest from their cells. My sense of smell was almost numb to the stench.

I was shoved into a stairway and began to climb, the chains around my ankles rattling on the stones. We twisted and turned through a labyrinth of passageways until we reached a massive wooden door. The soldier gripped the bolt and slid it free, then shoved the door open. The light from the courtyard was blinding. Instinctively I tried to shield my eyes from the light, but my shackled hands would not move. I could only twist my head and squint against the brilliance of the sun that exploded upon my darkened form.

They shoved me out into the opening. I stumbled, the chains hindering my legs as I sought to gain my balance. I was surrounded by confusion. The mob erupted in a deafening cry when they saw me thrust onto the stone platform. Gradually my eyes adjusted to the light as I sought to make sense of where I stood, what was going on. The chanting mob stretched below me into the streets. Behind me, surrounded by his military escorts, sat the governor, Pilate. He was surveying the scene, alternately examining me and the crowd, measuring their mood.

He raised his hand to silence the crowd. The leaders among the mob repeated the call, "Silence! Silence! Be quiet. The governor speaks!" Slowly the noise died down. The jostling crowd stood still, waiting to hear what Pilate would say.

It was then I became aware of another presence, another person standing opposite me on the platform. He was not bound with chains, as was I. He stood calmly, freely, poised, and unperturbed. His white robe glistened in the sun and fluttered gently in the breeze that swept across the scene. His face did not reflect the cynicism or worry of Pilate, nor the anger and vengeance of the mob. He turned slightly and looked at me, a look I had never seen. He did not just look at me, as so many others did. He looked into me. His gaze penetrated me, down into the substance of my soul. He seemed to know me, everything about me. It was as if his gaze summed up in total knowledge everything I had ever known, every thought I ever had. I felt as I had never felt before. In that moment I was known more thoroughly than anyone had ever known me before. He knew my fear, my doubt, my uncertainty, my ambition, my anger, everything. It seemed the meeting of our eyes lasted an eternity in an instant.

But Pilate was speaking, offering to free a prisoner to the crowd. A choice between the two of us: "Jesus," he said, "or Barabbas."

The crowd began to chant. It was my name they were chanting: "Barabbas! Barabbas! Barabbas!" crescendoing with each chant. They were calling for my release.

The governor was obviously disturbed. He rose from his judgment seat in apparent displeasure with the crowd's choice. He appealed to them. "What would you have me do then with Jesus?"

There was a moment of hesitation in the crowd, then a voice cried out, "Crucify! Crucify him!" And others joined in until they were screaming in unison: "Crucify! Crucify him!"

Pilate tried again to silence the crowd. He yelled at the crowd, "Why, what crime has he done?"

But they hardly seemed to hear, they only screamed the louder: "Crucify! Crucify!"

The governor turned, called for a basin of water, and rinsed his hands with obvious disgust. He withdrew, leaving us alone before the crowd, just the two of us, Jesus and I. The soldiers grabbed him, shoving him before them into the palace courtyard. The guard who had thrust me out of the dungeon gripped my arms, twisting my elbow up until I thought my arm would break. He unlocked the chains, dropping them from my wrists, then he released my feet. He did so with obvious contempt and then shoved me down the stairs into the midst of the mob.

I was not received with affection. The crowd cared nothing about me. As soon as I reached the bottom step they turned from me, taking no interest in me. They only wanted to have him killed. It was a twist of fate, his fate more than mine, that won my release. I sank back into the recesses of the crowd while they milled about, waiting for an hour or more. From within we could hear the soldiers mocking him, whipping him, berating him, laughing, and cursing.

Pilate reemerged, preceded by his guards. He took his place on the judgment seat and called for the soldiers to bring Jesus. When they brought him out he was almost unrecognizable. The Romans specialize in brutality. His faced was battered and bruised, his eyes swollen almost shut. Upon his head they had embedded a wreath of thorns that dug into the flesh. Blood dripped from his wounds. I think Pilate hoped that once they saw him so pitifully beaten they would have mercy and relent. Pilate restated his opinion: "I find no basis for a charge against him. Behold the man!" he cried. But the crowd was determined. They wanted nothing less than his death, and they shouted again, "Crucify! Crucify!"

They placed a roughly cut cross upon his shoulders and ordered him to carry it. He struggled beneath its weight, but pressed his shoulders against the splintered wood. The crowd parted and grew quiet, making a way for him to pass. He stumbled and fell. The beating had been severe. He was too weak. He seemed to speak to some women who were standing near him, weeping, bending toward him. I couldn't hear what he said. The soldiers grabbed a bystander, a strong heavyset man with broad shoulders, and commanded him to carry the cross. Slowly, the entire crowd followed outside the gate toward the place of crucifixion called Golgotha. I lingered along the edges, the people taking little notice of me.

Then I recognized my cell mates being dragged and pushed to the same hill. I heard their screams as the hammer fell, again and again, pounding the nails through their flesh and into the beams. They raised the crosses one at a time, my two companions on either side of the place where Jesus would die. Their bodies dangled from the nails. Then they hammered the nails through the hands and feet of Jesus. I heard every blow. *Those were my nails,* I thought. *That was to be me. I was the one to be crucified on that cross.* But he took the blows and uttered not a word. I looked at my hands. They were trembling. I was shaking. I had never trembled or shook like that before. But that day, I trembled.

They lifted him in the center and he hung between my two friends. I saw them speaking to one another. Painfully he raised his head, lifted himself against the nails that ground against his bones, drawing enough breath to speak. But again I couldn't hear what he said. I knew, even though his face was bloodied and bruised, he was looking into them like he looked into me. One of them continued to curse him like those at the front of the crowd. But the other, I could tell, even from my distance, the other seemed to draw breath and hope from him.

The crowd grew quiet. I could hear the women sobbing. Some of his accusers waited for him to die. The soldiers went about their callous business, some of them gambling near the place where he hung. Then Jesus spoke: "Father, forgive them . . ." I had never seen such love, such courage, such strength. I felt ashamed. He was praying for his assailants, for those who had accused him and lied, for those who beat him, for those who were killing him. I knew he was praying for me.

Father, too often I have resembled Barabbas rather than Jesus in my attitudes and actions. I find myself feeling resentful toward those who wrong me, wishing I could get even with them. Make me more like Jesus so that I can forgive those who treat me badly and love those who do not love me. Thank you that you loved me, even when I didn't love you, and that you paid the penalty for my sin by allowing Jesus to die in my place. I know that my life is not an accident. I could have easily died many times from an accident or a disease. Teach me your purpose for extending my life on earth. Help me to honor you with every breath I breathe.

QUESTIONS FOR REFLECTION

1. How would you describe the difference between Jesus and Barabbas? Who do you most resemble in your actions and attitudes, Jesus or Barabbas? Think of an example in your life that supports your answer. How can you be more like Jesus?

2. Imagine yourself standing before the cross of Jesus watching him suffer. It is not a pleasant thought. No one else is present but you and Jesus. Ask God to help you understand that the cross on which he suffered is your cross, created by your sin. The Bible tells us that Jesus died in your place to pay the penalty for your sins so you can live. Reflect on what God has done for you so that you might experience eternal life.

3. Every life is fragile. Think of a time in your life when you could have died. Do you think God spared your life? Why do you think he did it? What do you need to do today that will fulfill God's purpose for preserving your life on earth?

John 3:1–21; 7:50; 19:38–42

I GREW UP IN JERUSALEM, IN THE SHADOWS OF THE TEMPLE. FROM my earliest years I aspired to advance in Judaism. And advance I did, until I became a respected member of the Sanhedrin. My reputation was well known. I was on a first-name basis with the other council members, including the high priest. People on the streets recognized my importance by my robes, making way for me when I passed.

The first time I saw Jesus, he was only a boy. I was in my mid-twenties, attending the daily instruction in the temple. He was twelve. His cheeks were smooth, reflecting the complexion of childhood. His eyes were sharp. I remember those eyes. Even as a child they reflected his intelligence. How his eyes shown, fairly burned, with intelligence and integrity. Gamaliel, the great teacher, was my contemporary. He was brilliant, to be sure. But even Gamaliel paled in comparison with the genius we sensed in this child. He made some of our number nervous. He made us all uncomfortable. There is something unsettling about being in the presence of absolute genius. It threatens the security of our long held assumptions. Geniuses like that cannot help but question the unquestionable.

He posed questions to us, not with impudence or disrespect. His questions had the air of sincerity, an earnest search for the truth. His questions made our discussion seem trivial. We were apt to spend hours debating the fine points of the law: what activities were permissible on the Sabbath and what activities weren't, when we should wash and what method we should use in order to remain ceremonially clean, any number of similar details. We spent far more time discussing commentaries on the Scripture than we ever did discussing the Scripture itself. It was, as I look on it now, a way of keeping the real demands of knowing God at arm's length. As long as we kept our discussion on the fine points of tradition and ceremonial conduct, we didn't have to examine ourselves.

But his questions focused on God, on the nature of God and the heart of God. By the way he posed the questions and the way he answered ours, it was obvious this twelve-year-old boy knew God in personal terms we had never considered.

He asked about the Messiah, a subject we all entertained with keen interest. But he asked us to explain portions of Scripture regarding the Messiah we had never considered: Isaiah 53, Psalm 22, and others. We had never thought of these passages in terms of messianic prophecy. What could suffering and death have to do with the Promised One of Israel?

We were more than a little relieved when his mother and father, common Galileans, returned to retrieve him. Even his parents were perplexed and distraught over how to respond to him. His statement to them rang like the enigmatic questions he had posed to us: "Did you not know I must be about the things of my Father?" His parents did not understand his statement. Neither did we.

He represented no threat to us as a child. We easily dismissed him as a twelve-year-old boy. We doubted we would hear from him again, assuming he would pass into obscurity in some remote village of Galilee, a simple tradesman like his father. But I will never forget the impressions he made on me.

I didn't see him again until eighteen years later. I was in my forties. No longer a mere student, I had become a teacher of the law, a Pharisee, and a full-fledged member of the Sanhedrin. He was thirty. He had grown to the full stature of a man. The childlike cheeks had disappeared beneath a dark beard. His hands were still tender, but they showed the strength of one who knew manual labor. His eyes still burned with the intelligent fire I remembered from his youth, but they had more depth. He was more confident, more sure of himself. In fact, he fairly dripped confidence. Not the kind of confidence that is arrogant; rather, a confidence that simply has no doubt, the kind that comes from knowing what others do not know.

If he made us nervous when he was a child in the temple, he outright scared us now. The insights he had alluded to in Scripture almost two decades earlier were now well-formed convictions. How could we help but feel condemned when his teaching bypassed our superficial arguments and sank directly into the heart of knowing God?

I felt I had to know more. But my colleagues already viewed him as a threat. It would not serve me well to be publicly identified with him, to show unusual interest in him or his teachings. I waited for night to fall, when darkness would give me the kind of anonymity I needed to seek him out without being detected. He, of course, recognized me. He knew I was a ruler of the Jews, and marveled at my ignorance of spiritual things.

I complimented him as a teacher sent from God. But my flattery made no impression on him. He was totally unconcerned about my estimate of him or the estimation of others. He immediately turned the conversation to focus on my own spiritual ignorance. He knew, despite my theological training, I had no personal knowledge of the kingdom or of God's presence. He stunned me when he said,

"Truly I say to you, unless one is born again he cannot see the kingdom of God."

What did he mean? I was as puzzled by his statement, standing there in the darkness, as I had been when he spoke in the temple as a child. He always spoke in unexpected terms that unsettled traditional thought. How could one be born again? It isn't possible to reenter the womb! Once we are born our lives are set. We cannot begin again what is already begun. We cannot erase our past as if it never occurred.

I listened as he continued to explain. But his explanations only made me more confused. He said, "Unless one is born of water and the Spirit, he cannot enter into the kingdom of God. That which is born of the flesh is flesh; and that which is born of the Spirit is spirit. The wind blows where it wishes and you hear the sound of it, but do not know where it comes from and where it is going; so is everyone who is born of the Spirit."

He spoke of the *pneuma* of God, what we called in the Hebrew the *ruach,* or breath of God. Yes, I knew from my studies about the Spirit of God brooding over the waters of creation, of the Spirit empowering Moses and the people in the Exodus, of the Spirit anointing Saul and David, but all these were remote and long ago, special moments of God's intervention in our history. God's Spirit was too holy for us to consider in personal terms. I asked him, "How can these things be?"

He seemed shocked. "Are you a teacher of Israel and do not understand these things?" He made me feel as if I had failed the most elementary lessons of religious life. For decades I had studied the law. I knew all of its rules and regulations. I prided myself in obeying the law in its most minute detail. But I knew nothing about the Spirit of God.

"Truly," he said, "I say to you, we speak that which we know, and bear witness of that which we have seen; and you do not receive our witness."

Now I was really confused. Why did he speak in the plural? He spoke of a spiritual knowledge of God that transcended theology and religion. He had seen things I could never imagine, things of God the rest of us could not comprehend. I remember distinctly what he said: "As Moses lifted up the serpent, even so must the Son of Man be lifted up, that whoever believes in him may have eternal life. For God so loved the world that he gave his only begotten Son, that whoever believes in him should not perish but have eternal life."

These words remained a mystery to me until later, after he was executed. The day he was executed was a dark day, literally. It all started in darkness. We were summoned from our beds to the temple area to convene the council. This had never been done. It was not even legal according to our law. But we went. Caiaphas had called. We dared not challenge the high priest. We did not respect him. He was more a political pawn than a spiritual leader, but he was powerful.

It was cold that morning. I rubbed my hands together for warmth as I made my way to the council chamber. I passed a fire outside, surrounded by a huddle of commoners warming themselves, a motley mix of soldiers, women, and a few Galileans. I thought I saw one of his twelve disciples shivering there beside the fire. But he kept his head down so that I could not see him clearly.

Once inside we sat silently as they brought him before us. In the shadows of that predawn assembly, the lights of the lamps reflecting from his face, the words he spoke to me in the night kept ringing in my ears. "For God so loved ... he gave his only begotten Son." Caiaphas was anxious. His eyes roamed constantly about the room while he shifted his body weight in the chair of judgment. His knuckles turned white as he angrily gripped the arms of the chair.

One after another they brought in witnesses against Jesus. They lied. We all knew it. Even so, none of their testimony was sufficient for the condemnation Caiaphas sought. Finally two witnesses testified to his words: "I am able to destroy the temple of God and raise it again in three days." Of course, many of us knew these were not the words Jesus spoke. We had heard him when he said, "Destroy this temple and I will raise it again in three days." But it was close enough for Caiaphas.

Caiaphas leaped to his feet. He sensed he had him in his grasp. He spoke directly toward Jesus: "Do you make no answer? What is it that these men are testifying against you?" But Jesus did not answer him. He was not flustered. In the midst of that tumultuous moment, he was the only one who was completely calm. He merely fastened his eyes on the priest, those eyes I had seen in the child and again in the night visit. It drove Caiaphas into a fury.

He pounded his fist on the arm of his chair as he shouted at him, "I adjure you by the living God, that you tell us whether you are the Christ, the Son of God!"

Then Jesus spoke in a calm, measured voice that filled the room: "You have said it yourself; nevertheless I tell you, hereafter you shall see the Son of Man sitting at the right hand of power and coming on the clouds of heaven." As masters of the Scripture we recognized his words as messianic prophecies from Psalm 110 and Daniel 7. There could be no dispute in what he meant. He had claimed to be the Christ, the promised Messiah.

A smirk spread across the high priest's face. He knew he had him. Feigning shock and indignation, Caiaphas almost gleefully ripped his robes in a display of righteous rage and cried, "He has blasphemed! What further need do we have of witnesses? Behold you have now heard the blasphemy; what do you think?"

All around me I heard my colleagues shouting. They jumped to their feet and waved their fists in the air. "He is deserving of death!" they cried. They were so enraged that they did not notice I remained seated, hidden within the ranks of what had now become a mob. I looked to my left between the shaking garments that surrounded me and saw my friend Joseph of Arimathea seated as I was. His head was down, his eyes fixed in a blank stare of dismay. I could no longer see Jesus. But I heard them spitting upon him, striking him with their fists, slapping him about the face. The noise subsided only after the guards grabbed him and ushered him out to Herod and Pilate. He was automatically referred to the Roman authorities. Only they could carry out the capital punishment our council was demanding. We were, after all, subject to Roman rule. We had only limited rights, which the Romans tolerated but rarely respected. I did not see him again until he was dead.

I did not attend the trial before Pilate, though I could hear the echoes of the mob from my house. Neither did I go out to the site of execution beyond the gates of the city when they crucified him. I had seen enough. I was ashamed. I had not spoken for him. I kept silent and, by my silence, acquiesced to the sentence of death he received.

The day wore on. It was afternoon. The streets were quiet. Almost everyone had emptied them to watch the crucifixion. It was difficult for me to understand this strange, morbid attraction people have to witness bloodshed and torture. Some parents had even taken their children.

Someone was knocking on my door, an insistent, desperate knocking. I fearfully opened the door slightly, and then swung it wide to welcome my friend Joseph of Arimathea. Joseph was wealthy, a man of influence in Jerusalem. We had become friends many years before. As a layman, he had a keen interest in religion and often asked me questions of the Scripture. We had become fast friends. He had become a member of the council as a member of the secular nobility in Jerusalem, an aristocrat with influence among the Romans. I knew Joseph secretly believed in Jesus, but, like me, he feared the others, the council members and the high priest. It would not have been profitable for him to be known in Jerusalem as a disciple of Jesus.

His hands trembled as he entered. He told me had been at Golgotha, watching as they crucified him. He tried to describe the horror of the torturous scene, but tears welled up in his eyes and his voice broke. Then he turned to me with a desperate look.

"I've decided I must do something," he said. "I have been cowardly and timid while they have condemned and tortured him. I have betrayed him in life. I must do something for him in death. I have decided to go to Pilate to claim his body so I can bury him in my tomb."

I looked at him with unbelief.

"Will you go with me?" he asked.

"Is he dead?" I asked.

"Yes. They made a wreath of thorns and pressed it into his brow. They nailed him to a cross with huge spikes through his hands and feet. He had been beaten badly with whips and clubs. He struggled to breathe while the weight of his body pulled against the nails. I heard his last breath. He cried out, 'Father, into thy hands I commend my spirit.' Then he sank against the nails and was motionless.

"Something must be done quickly, if we are to claim his body and give him a decent burial. Otherwise, his body will be taken down and destroyed with the common criminals. Will you help me?"

"What about his disciples?" I asked. "Won't they claim the body?"

"No," Joseph answered. "His disciples have disappeared. They have all forsaken him. Besides, Pilate would not likely grant his body to any of them, common Galileans. Only you, as a respected teacher among the Jews, and I, an influential businessman, could possibly persuade Pilate to give us his body. What do you think?"

"I don't know," I said. "Why should we risk rejection now that he's dead? It's over. We have our future to consider."

Joseph was slow in speaking. His look alone was sufficient to fill me with embarrassment and shame. "Even though, as you say, he is dead, I still believe he was the Messiah. I'm no theologian. I'm not sure what all that means. But you and I both know he did not deserve to die.

He was the only pure human being I have ever known. If you won't go with me, then I must go alone."

He turned to leave, obviously disappointed, and I felt disgusted with my response.

"Wait!" I called, "Let me get my coat. I will go with you. We may regret it later, but you are right; it must be done."

A smile spread across Joseph's face. His eyes gleamed. That look on Joseph's face I will never forget it. That look was reward enough, to see my friend genuinely grateful, to feel the comradeship between us, linked together in doing what was right, even though it might cost us dearly.

Pilate seemed glad to get rid of the body. We could tell he was disgusted with the whole mess. In fact, he seemed genuinely grieved about condemning Jesus to crucifixion. He did not argue or resist. I think he was grateful that someone stepped forward to claim the body. His secretary quickly wrote a document transferring the corpse to Joseph's care, then affixed his royal seal with his own signature.

We stopped in the market on our way outside the city gates. Though the markets were still open, there were few shoppers. Many had gone to see the executions. The merchants seemed nervous. No wind blew. The dark clouds hung low over the land, like a suffocating canopy of death. Joseph bought the most expensive and exquisite linen cloth available in which to wrap his body. I purchased myrrh and aloes.

We hurried, knowing we had little time before the Sabbath. Some of the women helped us. We were not able to complete the preparation as we would have liked, but we did the best we could and laid him in Joseph's tomb. We stood there for a few moments together, Joseph and I, after the servants had rolled the stone in place over the opening. We didn't speak. His blood had stained our garments and our hands. The two of us stood there, bloodstained, and wept.

Father, I find it easier to go through the motions of religion than to nurture a personal relationship of faith with you. Forgive me when my faith becomes rote and routine. Keep my faith alive and fresh with a daily trust in you. Forgive me for hiding my faith and not speaking up when I should. Show me how to express my faith so that others will be attracted to a personal faith in Jesus Christ.

QUESTIONS FOR REFLECTION

1. What is the difference between religious observance and personal faith? How would you describe your religious experience?

2. Are you happy with the way your life is going? Does your religion seem dry, empty, and lifeless? Jesus has promised to change your life if you will truly trust in him. If you would like to make a new start, pray now that Jesus Christ will create in you a new heart and give you a living personal relationship with him.

3. What does it mean to be a disciple of Jesus Christ? Would you describe yourself as a disciple? How do others know you are a disciple of Jesus?

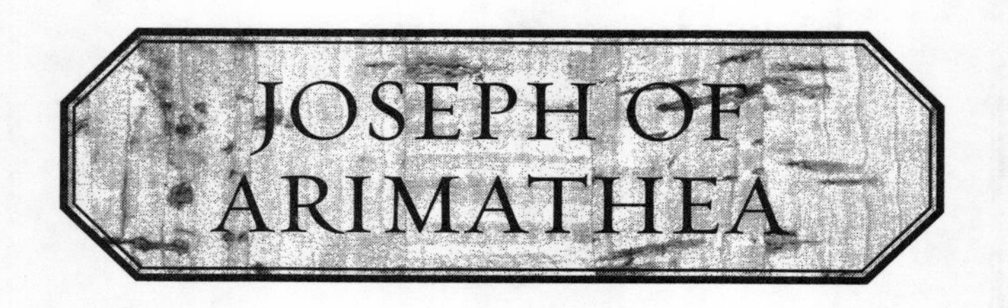

Matthew 27:57–60
Mark 15:43–46
Luke 23:50–54
John 19:38–42

I WAS A MEMBER OF THE SANHEDRIN THAT CONDEMNED JESUS. Unlike the majority of the Sanhedrin, I was not a native of Jerusalem. I grew up in Arimathea, a village more accurately called Ramah Arimathaim, the home of the great prophet and judge Samuel. It was impossible to grow up in that city without absorbing the history and heritage of the place. It was in my home village, only twenty miles northwest of Jerusalem, that Elkanah and Hannah had prayed for a son and given birth to Samuel. After his training in the temple, Samuel made Ramah Arimathaim his home. I could feel the presence of the sage who anointed Saul as the first king of Israel, and his successor, King David.

Growing up in such a place created in me an expectancy for the Messiah, the One who would fulfill God's promise to the house of David to raise up a king who would reign eternally on David's throne.

It was in Arimathea that I made my first wealth. I then moved to Jerusalem because of the greatly expanded opportunities for investment and business. The religious politics, however, never appealed to me.

The council members were glad to count me among their number because of my influence. I was well known and respected by the Romans. Though they had little respect for a Jew, they respected money and success, both of which I had in large measure. I enjoyed easy access both to the courts of the Jews and to the palace of Pilate.

Although I was a member of the Sanhedrin, I was not a theologian. My talent was business. That was what landed me a place on the council. Every enterprise I started and every business in which I invested prospered. I faithfully worshiped in the temple and kept all the laws of my Jewish faith, but the disputed questions of the law and of prophecy I left to others.

I listened to the rabbis. Most of them were boring, often losing me in their speculative comparisons of commentary on the Scripture. My mind wandered often to the latest and most promising business deals upon which I was working. Occasionally, I even fell asleep during their long expositions.

Jesus was different. The common people called him rabbi, though he had no credentials. Even my good friend in the council, Nicodemus, referred to him by that term. But he spoke like no rabbi I had ever heard.

He did not quote commentaries. He made no display of his knowledge of obscure references. Absent from his teaching were the legalistic gymnastics, which drove so many of us mad, the infuriating ability of lawyers to twist the issue and manipulate the argument, to spin a complex web of logic around details of definition.

He spoke simply and directly in words everyone could understand. I liked him. He had refreshing integrity about him, a quiet but powerful presence. The young Samuel, I thought, born of his mother's prayer, raised in the temple as a child, called personally by God at an early age, must have been more like Jesus than the professional clergy and lawyers.

On several occasions I heard Jesus speak. I became a believer, though secretly. How could I defend my faith among the other council members? My faith was simple, childlike, a faith of the heart, not one that could withstand their withering attacks. So I kept it to myself.

I knew of the council's desire to trap Jesus. They felt threatened by him, fearing he would incite riots among the common population that would precipitate an even tighter stranglehold by the Romans. The authority of the council had already been reduced. Once it had held civil power over the entire region, but since the death of Herod its jurisdiction had eroded to Judea and was limited to minor issues. An uprising of the people could result in the absolute abolishment of the Sanhedrin by the overwhelming force of Rome. In spite of its aristocratic pride, the council knew they existed only by permission of the Romans and were dependent upon their tolerance.

In all honesty, I was shocked when the council suddenly convened to condemn Jesus to death. I knew Caiaphas, the high priest, was devious. But I had underestimated the treachery of the men who claimed to be spiritual leaders of Israel. As a businessman I knew how to be hard-nosed, how to negotiate a deal. But the back-stabbing deceit I experienced on that night exceeded anything I had known in the secular world. Business prospers only in a climate of trust and mutual benefit. Religion, it seemed, could descend into the depths of the darkest nature of man. The ends justified whatever means necessary to rid themselves of Jesus.

I abstained from the vote to condemn him. The rest, most of them at least, were on their feet calling him a blasphemer and shouting for his death. They behaved more like a mob than a council, whipped into a frenzy by Caiaphas himself.

I followed the events closely through the day: his trial before Pilate, the demand for Barabbas to be released instead of Jesus, his condemnation and torture, the sad wailing walk through sorrowful streets outside the city to the hill called the skull. It was there they crucified him, driving nails through his hands and feet and raising him above the heads of the crowd where all could watch him writhe in agony. I did not weep like the women, nor did I scoff like his accusers who laughed and demanded he save himself from the cross if he was indeed the Son of God. I stood stone-faced, emotionless, watching, until the final hour when he yielded his spirit to God.

There was little I could do. But I could at least claim his body and give him a decent burial. I determined that though he had been abandoned in life by even his closest disciples, I would not abandon him in death. It was there, in that moment, that my mind was suddenly set in undeterred determination. I would go to Pilate and claim his body. I would bury him in my tomb, which I had prepared for my own burial.

But I needed help. I could not do it all alone. That is when I sought out my friend Nicodemus to accompany me to Pilate and to help me bury Jesus. I knew Nicodemus felt about him as I did. We had secretly talked on many occasions since Jesus had come to Jerusalem. Neither of us, however, had spoken up for him in the council. At first Nicodemus was unwilling to go with me. But he soon changed his mind. I knew he would.

Pilate was only too glad to relieve himself of the body. Once he was assured of his death, he immediately gave me written custody of his corpse, sealed with the imprint of the governor's ring.

We stopped only momentarily to buy the necessary spices and the linen cloth in which we would bury him. I knew the merchant who owned the most exclusive and expensive textile store in the city. I had traded there many times. I asked for the most expensive cloth available. Money was no object. I demanded the best; nothing else was worthy of holding the body of the one I believed to be the Messiah of God. I chose a rare herringbone twill weave of the finest flax. It was the only one he had in stock. Nicodemus purchased spices weighing upward to seventy-five pounds. We would spare no expense or effort to give Jesus a decent burial.

When we returned to the place of crucifixion, all three of the victims were dead. The soldiers had broken the legs of the two thieves who hung to his right and left. Their bodies hung motionless from the nails that held them to the wooden crosses. The crowd had dispersed. Only a few women remained, silently weeping near the foot of the center cross that held Jesus.

The soldiers were taking the bodies down, ruthlessly ripping the criminal to Jesus' left from the cross member that held him. They were about to do the same with Jesus. I stopped them. At first they dismissed me as a Jew, but I held the paper clearly in their sight so they could see the insignia of the governor's seal. This halted them in their tracks. The soldier in charge quickly read over the document entrusting Jesus' body to my possession. He raised his eyes and looked squarely in my face. I was surprised at his expression. He was a Roman soldier accustomed to the brutality of war and criminal executions, but his features were soft. His eyes were moist. "Surely," he said, "this man was the Son of God. I have never seen a man die like this man died. I am glad you are claiming his body."

It was not easy taking Jesus down from the cross where he hung. Although he was dead, we tried to be gentle in our efforts to release his hands and feet from the nails. By the time we lowered him to the ground, Nicodemus and I were both covered in blood. Blood was everywhere. His entire body was covered with lash wounds from the Roman flagrum. The pieces of bone tied at the end of the three leather straps had repeatedly dug into his flesh when he was whipped, biting deep and ripping gashes in his shoulders, back, chest, and legs. I had seen criminals whipped by the Romans before. It is a ghastly thing. It seemed the soldiers who lashed Jesus were particularly savage. The loss of blood from the scourge wounds alone would have killed him.

Nicodemus and I carried him to the cemetery. I carried his head and shoulders with my hands gripping his arms. I saw the scalp wounds from the thorns which penetrated deep into his skull. They bled profusely. Nicodemus carried his legs and feet. We stumbled a couple of times. He must have weighed approximately one hundred and seventy-five pounds. Neither of us was young. But we carried him nonetheless. The women who followed brought the cloth and spices.

The sun was already setting, so time was short. We could not continue the burial process after dark. This would violate the Sabbath laws of Judaism. We had to hurry. When we reached the tomb, the shadows were already long and growing darker by the minute. We did not have time to wash his body. Blood still seeped from the wounds in his hands, feet, side, and head.

The women waited outside while we took his body into the tomb. We gently unrolled half the linen cloth lengthwise on the bench where we would place his body. Then we lifted him and laid him on the cloth. Nicodemus took a narrow strip of cloth and tied his feet together while I tied his hands draped across his abdomen. Then Nicodemus held his jaw shut while I tied a cloth around the jaw and over his head to hold his jaw in position awaiting rigor mortis. His face was bloody and bruised. I gently closed his eyes with my own hands. Those eyes that in life had looked with such piercing power into the inner heart of men were now vacant in death, staring into some unknown distance. I pulled from my purse two leptons, Roman coins, and placed them on his eyes to hold his eyes closed.

Nicodemus and I then pulled the remaining cloth over his head and covered the length of his body. Hurriedly we placed the spices around him. Then, for a moment, we stood and studied his burial form. What we had done was hasty and incomplete. But, under the circumstances, it was the best we could do. Blood was already soaking through some portions of the cloth that covered him. I asked Nicodemus to pray, which he did, and then we left.

Once outside, I ordered my servants to seal the tomb with a large boulder. Only a faint glow remained in the west where the sun had already sunk beneath the horizon. Darkness was gathering, a deep darkness that seemed to penetrate every recess of my heart. My feet were heavy as I made my way home that night.

The darkness I felt that day remained until I heard from his closest followers the events that followed, and eventually saw him for myself along with five hundred others. He knew all along what he was doing. He knew he had to die. He knew I would bury him. And he knew he would conquer death. The tomb I had constructed for my own death has become a monument to eternal life for everyone who believes.

Father, help me honor you in all my business dealings. Help me be honest and truthful, refusing to take advantage of others even when I am given the opportunity. Thank you for allowing me the privilege of giving a portion of my income to benefit the church and Christian causes. This gives me great pleasure, and I thank you for providing the means for me to give. Help me find other believers in my work, so we can encourage each other to be faithful to you.

QUESTIONS FOR REFLECTION

1. How do you bring your faith into your business? What business decisions do you make differently because of your faith in Christ? How do you treat people differently from how you would if you were not a believer?

2. How do the people you work with know you are a Christian? Ask God to provide a Christian friend in your place of work so you can encourage each other in your walk with Christ.

3. How do you honor God with your income? What portion of your income do you give to your church and to Christian causes? Does your generosity reflect a deep trust in God and love for him?

SALOME

Matthew 20:20–28; 27:56
Mark 15:40; 16:1
John 19:25

WE WERE A SIMPLE CLOSE-KNIT FISHING FAMILY: MY HUSBAND, Zebedee, myself, and our two sons, James and John. For generations our family had lived on the shore of Galilee in the small village of Bethsaida. The name of our village reflected our heritage. It literally meant "House of Fishing." Zebedee learned the fishing business from his father, and he from his. The arts of building boats, mending nets, and catching fish were highly prized family traditions.

I still have images in my mind of those simple days: the sight of the sails silhouetted against the sunsets on Galilee; the voices of my husband and my sons laughing with excitement while the day's catch thrashed in their nets; the waves cresting on the sea, sighing upon the shore, washing the sand with white fingers of foam.

There is something about the sea that is close to God. Maybe it is the rhythmic crash of the waves upon the shore, echoing the eternal heartbeat of God. Or maybe it is because the waves had lapped the Galilean shore centuries before we were born, before our fishing village was formed, before the region was known as Galilee, and even before our ancestor Abraham was called from Ur of the Chaldeans. Maybe that was what made my family sensitive to spiritual things. How could anyone listen to the sound of the sea for a lifetime and make their living by harvesting its fruit without having a sense of the eternal?

Of course we weren't alone. We were close friends with others who plied the depths off the shore of Galilee. We depended on each other and we were all dependent upon the weather and the natural resources God provided day by day.

My sons were good friends with Simon and Andrew. They fished together, worked together, and played together. How many times I cooked for those boys! How they could eat! Piles of fish and stacks of bread vanished from the table when they gathered in our home. The room filled with laughter as they mimicked one another's most embarrassing moments: Simon drawing the nets with such enthusiasm he lost his balance and fell headlong into the water with the fish; James and John lifting their oars as they rowed so that with each stroke they drenched Andrew, who was seated in the rear holding fast to the rudder, growing angrier with each dousing. They literally rolled on the floor laughing. It was no use trying to reprove their crude manners when they spoke with mouths stuffed full with food. Those are wonderful moments in my memory.

I listened when they grew quiet under the cloud of serious discussion. Inevitably their talks turned to the imminent appearance of the Messiah. Simon was skeptical. He had little patience for such speculation. Unlike the rest, he was already married and more concerned about building his own business to provide for his wife and her mother who lived with them. But his brother, Andrew, and my youngest, John, . . . how their eyes would sparkle and glisten as they talked about the Messiah! I understood. I cannot put my finger on it. I don't know why we had this overwhelming anticipation for the Promised One. It was like the sea, something that communed with our soul and awakened us to the possibility.

I remember the day everything changed. Andrew and John had gone off to listen to a visiting preacher, a young man, slightly older than they were, but still barely thirty years old. His fame was widespread and everyone was turning out to hear him. They called him John.

When they returned, their faces were glowing, their eyes ablaze with excitement. They were convinced they had found the Messiah. The preacher had pointed Jesus out to them and told them that he was the "Lamb of God that takes away the sins of the world." They had spent the entire evening with him and were completely convinced. "No one," they said, "ever spoke like this man!" They even persuaded Simon to go back with them.

After their second trip, Andrew and John returned more convinced than ever that they had met the One Israel had been waiting for. Even James joined in their enthusiasm. Simon, however, seemed perplexed. From what the boys said, Jesus had taken a special interest in Simon, even giving him a new name, "Peter," a stone. Of course, everyone knows him by that name now, but it seemed strange then, especially since Simon was not the most spiritually inclined among them. The others joked with him and said Jesus called him that because he was so hardheaded!

It was not long after this that Jesus came to our village. As usual, the men were working near their boats. Simon, always hoping to enlarge his catch, was tirelessly casting his net into the sea, trying to snare some fish from the shallow waters. Andrew was helping him. My boys, James and John, were working with my husband mending the nets for the next day's catch. Torn and threadbare nets are useless in the fishing business. We learned long ago the value of nets that are strong and well-mended to draw a thrashing catch of fish from the sea.

That is when they left—all of them: Simon, Andrew, James, and John. Jesus told them to follow him and he would make them "fishers of men." I must admit Zebedee was not entirely happy about losing our sons from the fishing business. But I was thrilled! What mother wouldn't be? My sons were going to spend their lives learning from the chosen Messiah of Israel! I assured Zebedee we could hire others to help him with the fishing. He grunted and complained, but gave in. I knew he would. He is a good man.

I felt the most for Simon's young wife. She was left to care for her mother while Simon was gone. But we reassured her. We were close friends, almost family, and we would not let her suffer. She came to my house often and we talked. As an older woman, I felt it my duty to befriend her and help her understand more clearly the significance of what was happening. I knew deep in my soul that we were living in the most significant moment in history, the fulfillment of all the prophecies and the activity of God to redeem mankind to himself. She was a willing learner, a gentle and kind young woman, just the woman a man like Simon needed. After Jesus visited their home and healed her mother, she was as convinced as anyone. She gladly gave up her husband so that he could follow the Messiah. It was interesting to watch her blossom in her faith and grow in her understanding. Of course, since the resurrection, she has been traveling all over the world with Peter, and others know she is a wonderful disciple in her own right.

I must confess, however, like everyone else, I did not understand the real reason Jesus came. We all imagined he would become a powerful ruler. No one who met him could doubt he had the ability. He could have been a king, a more powerful king than Alexander the Great, or Caesar Augustus, let alone the petty rulers of Palestine, like Herod and Pilate. How we hungered for a ruler like Jesus, someone so wise and kind and just, someone who could stand up to the Romans and the corrupt rulers among the Jews.

My ambition ran ahead of my understanding. That is when I sought him out and asked him what must have seemed a childish question. I asked him for the favor of having my sons sit on his right and left whenever he established his kingdom. Actually, I never intended it selfishly. I just wanted him to know how deeply and truly I believed in him, that I was ready for my sons to stand by him and to serve him in any way he chose. Is it wrong for a mother to have such ambitions for her children? I hope not.

His answer confused me. So many of his answers seemed confusing at the time. Of course, I understand now what he meant. But I simply had no way to comprehend what he meant then. He said, "You don't know what you are asking. Can you drink the cup I drink?" Both of my boys were standing nearby and they spoke up without hesitation, promising they indeed could drink the cup he drank.

I remember the look on his face. He looked sad. He seemed to feel sorry for us, because we had no understanding what he was speaking about. I could see the love in his eyes when he told us, "You will indeed drink from my cup, but to sit at my right and my left is not for me to grant."

It was startling to me to discover what a furor we had set off. The other ten of his disciples were incensed at my question and at James and John for wanting the honor of sitting at his right and left. They squabbled among themselves like children. That is when he interrupted them and taught them an unforgettable lesson. He told them that the world equates greatness with power and position. Those who are important in the world's view are able to command and control those who serve them. But, he said, it is entirely different in the kingdom of God. In his kingdom the greatest is a servant and the one who is first is a slave. He was always turning things upside down. Then a cloud seemed to sweep over his face, his eyes focused in some distant place we could not see. His lips almost mumbled, as if he were speaking to himself and no longer to those of us who were standing near him. He said, "It is just like the Son of Man, who did not come to be served, but to serve, and to give his life a ransom for many."

Of course, I know now what he meant by the "cup." He was referring to his own suffering, the torture, the beating, and the crucifixion. I am sure when he looked into the eyes of my sons he knew they too would suffer. It has been many years now since James died. He was my oldest. He was the first of Jesus' followers to be killed. Herod had him arrested and, without the benefit of a trial, executed him with the sword.

Do you know what it is like to be a mother and watch your son die? I do. Even though James was a grown man, he was still my son. I remember the day I gave birth to him, the months I nursed him, the feel of his little body going limp with sleep at my breast. I remember his beaming eyes as a child, his little belly laugh whenever he found a crab on the shore, how he ran when the waves washed around him, tickling his feet. I remember his childhood, and his adolescence, his broadening shoulders, his deeply tanned skin from hours in the sun helping Zebedee with the day's catch of fish. Those memories never leave a mother's mind. And his absence is painful every day.

But I know too that Jesus gave him the wish I wished for him, to drink of the same cup the Messiah drank. I believe he is with him now in heaven, sitting at his right hand, just like I asked, raised in the same way Jesus was raised to live forever.

My youngest, John, still lives. All the rest have died in one manner or another, most of them martyred for their witness concerning Jesus. But John remains. He was the most sensitive, the most introspective of his followers. He has always been that way, even as a child. He liked mending the nets so he could have time to think and visit quietly with friends.

The world hasn't changed, you know. We are still ruled by unjust and corrupt rulers. We still hear stories of violence and hatred. But the world within our hearts is changed. Jesus showed us how to live in this world, with tenderness, honesty, compassion, and faith. He taught us how to serve each other and look out for what is best for our neighbor. And he demonstrated to us, without any shadow of a doubt, our destiny beyond death, to live forever with him in the kingdom not made with hands.

I was there. I watched when he died, along with the other women: Mary his mother, Mary the wife of Clopas, and Mary Magdalene. We all watched with horror as they tortured him to death. And we all went early on the first day of the week discovering the empty tomb and the first evidence of his resurrection.

Father, sometimes I find it hard to understand why you would allow someone close to me to die. Help me to experience your peace that sustains me in the loss, and shape my life so I may be a greater blessing to others. I pray that those I love the most on this earth will experience a personal faith in Jesus Christ so that they honor him and love him. Help me accept suffering and hardships when they come in such a way that others may trust in you.

QUESTIONS FOR REFLECTION

1. How has God helped you through your greatest personal loss?

2. How are you communicating your faith to your family? How are you encouraging them to believe?

3. If you are a parent, what is your greatest ambition for your children? What do you desire the most for those who are closest to you?